# GRE® Exam
# Vocabulary Flashcards,
# Second Edition

**Other Kaplan Books on Graduate School Admissions**

Get Into Graduate School: A Strategic Approach

GRE Exam 2007 Edition: Comprehensive Program

GRE Exam 2007 Edition: Premier Program (CD-ROM)

GRE Exam Subject Test: Biology, 2007–2008 Edition

GRE Exam Subject Test: Psychology, Third Edition

GRE Exam Verbal Workbook, Fourth Edition

GMAT Math Workbook, Fifth Edition

GRE Exam Math Workbook

# GRE® Exam

## Vocabulary Flashcards, Second Edition

KAPLAN

Contributing Editors: Susan Kaplan, Matt Fidler
Editorial Director: Jennifer Farthing
Editor: Megan Gilbert
Production Editor: Caitlin Ostrow
Production Artist: Joe Budenholzer
Cover Designer: Carly Schnur



Published by Kaplan Publishing, a division of Kaplan, Inc.
888 Seventh Ave.
New York, NY 10106


Printed in the United States of America

August 2006
10 9 8 7 6 5 4

ISBN-13: 978-1-4195-4194-0
ISBN-10: 1-4195-4194-3

# HOW TO USE THIS BOOK

Kaplan's *GRE® Exam Vocabulary Flashcards* is perfectly designed to help you learn 500 of the hardest, most essential GRE vocabulary words in a quick, easy, and fun way. On the front of each flashcard you'll find a GRE vocabulary word along with its part of speech and pronunciation. On the back you'll find the word's definition and synonyms, as well as a sample sentence with the vocabulary word in action. Feel free to skip over words once you've mastered them: Just clip or fold back the corner of the flashcard so that you can flip right by it on your next pass through the book. Kaplan's *GRE® Exam Vocabulary Flashcards* is packed with the toughest GRE vocabulary so you can flip your way to a higher score. Don't forget to flip the book over for the other half of the 500 hardest GRE words.

Good luck, and happy flipping!

## ABASE

verb (uh <u>bays</u>)

a gentle breeze; something airy or unsubstantial

The *zephyr* from the ocean made the intense heat on the beach bearable for the sunbathers.

Synonyms: breath; draft

to humble; disgrace

My intention was not to *abase* the comedian.

Synonyms: demean, humiliate

**ZEPHYR**

noun (zeh fuhr)

## ABATE

verb (uh bayt)

the point of culmination; peak

The diva considered her appearance at the Metropolitan Opera to be the *zenith* of her career.

Synonyms: acme; pinnacle

to reduce in amount, degree, or severity

As the hurricane's force *abated*, the winds dropped and the sea became calm.

Synonyms: ebb; lapse; let up; moderate; relent; slacken; subside; wane

**ZENITH**

noun (zee nihth)

**ABDICATE**

verb (<u>aab</u> duh kayt)

someone passionately devoted to a cause

The religious *zealot* had no time for those who failed to share his strong beliefs.

Synonyms: enthusiast; fanatic; militant; radical

to give up a position, right, or power

With the angry mob clamoring outside the palace, the king *abdicated* his throne and fled.

Synonyms: cede; relinquish; resign; quit; yield

**ZEALOT**

noun (zeh luht)

## ABERRANT

adj (uh ber unt)

passion, excitement

She brought her typical *zeal* to the project, sparking enthusiasm in the other team members.

Synonyms: ardency; fervor; fire; passion

deviating from what is normal or expected

> Since he had been a steady, cheerful worker for many years, his fellow postal workers did not expect his *aberrant* burst of rage.

Synonyms: abnormal; anomalous; deviant; divergent; errant; irregular

**ZEAL**

adj (zeehl)

## ABEYANCE

noun (uh <u>bay</u> uhns)

to join together

As soon as the farmer had *yoked* his oxen together, he began to plow the fields.

Synonyms: bind; harness; pair

temporary suppression or suspension

The baseball game was held in *abeyance* while it continued to rain.

Synonyms: deferral; delay; dormancy; postponement; remission

**YOKE**

verb (yohk)

a fear or hatred of foreigners or strangers

Countries in which *xenophobia* is prevalent often have more restrictive immigration policies than countries that are more open to foreign influences.

Synonyms: bigotry; chauvinism; prejudice

## ABJURE

verb (aab jur)

to reject; abandon formally

The spy *abjured* his allegiance to the United States when he defected to Russia.

Synonyms: forswear; recall; recant; retract; take back

**XENOPHOBIA**

noun (zee nuh foh bee uh)

# ABSCOND

verb (aab <u>skahnd</u>)

a ghost or specter; a ghost of a living person seen just before his or her death

Gideon thought he saw a *wraith* late one night as he sat vigil outside his great uncle's bedroom door.

Synonyms: apparition; bogeyman; phantasm; shade; spirit

to leave secretly

The patron *absconded* from the restaurant without paying his bill.

Synonyms: decamp; escape; flee

**WRAITH**

noun (rayth)

## ACME

noun (aak me)

undisciplined, unrestrained, reckless

The townspeople were outraged by the *wanton* display of disrespect when they discovered the statue of the town founder covered in graffiti.

Synonyms: capricious; lewd; licentious

highest point; summit; the highest level or degree attainable

Just when he reached the *acme* of his power, the dictator was overthrown.

Synonyms: apex; peak; summit

**WANTON**

adj (wahn tuhn)

## ADULTERATE

verb (uh duhl tuhr ayt)

sickly pale

The sick child had a *wan* face, in contrast to her rosy-cheeked sister.

Synonyms: ashen; sickly

to make impure

The restaurateur made his ketchup last longer by *adulterating* it with water.

Synonyms: debase; doctor; load

**WAN**

adj (wahn)

## ADVOCATE

verb (<u>aad</u> vuh kayt)

talkative, speaking easily, glib

The *voluble* man and his reserved wife proved the old saying that opposites attract.

Synonyms: loquacious; verbose

to speak in favor of

The vegetarian *advocated* a diet containing no meat.

Synonyms: back; champion; support

**VOLUBLE**

adj (vahl yuh buhl)

## AERIE

noun (ayr ee) (eer ee)

easily aroused or changeable; lively or explosive

His *volatile* personality made it difficult to predict his reaction to anything.

Synonyms: capricious; erratic; fickle; inconsistent; inconstant; mercurial; temperamental

a nest built high in the air; an elevated, often secluded dwelling

Perched high among the trees, the eagle's *aerie* was filled with eggs.

Synonyms: perch; stronghold

**VOLATILE**

adj (vah luh tuhl)

## AESTHETIC

adj (ehs theh tihk)

to abuse verbally, berate

*Vituperating* someone is never a constructive way to effect change.

Synonyms: castigate; reproach; scold

concerning the appreciation of beauty

The *Aesthetic* Movement regarded the pursuit of beauty to be the only true purpose of art.

Synonyms: artistic; tasteful

**VITUPERATE**

verb (vih too puhr ayt)

## AFFECTED

adj (uh fehk tihd)

thick and adhesive, like a slow-flowing fluid

Most *viscous* liquids, like oil or honey, become even thicker as they are cooled down.

Synonyms: gelatinous; glutinous; thick

phony, artificial

The *affected* hairdresser spouted French phrases, though she had never been to France.

Synonyms: insincere; pretentious; put-on

**VISCOUS**

adj (vih skuhs)

## AGGRANDIZE

verb (uh graan diez) (aa gruhn diez)

vitality and energy

The *vim* with which she worked so early in the day explained why she was so productive.

Synonyms: force; power

to increase in power, influence and reputation

The supervisor sought to *aggrandize* himself by claiming that the achievements of his staff were actually his own.

Synonyms: amplify; augment; elevate

**VIM**

noun (vihm)

## ALACRITY

noun (uh laak crih tee)

---

a change or variation; ups and downs

Investors must be prepared for *vicissitudes* in the stock market.

Synonyms: inconstancy; mutability

promptness, cheerful readiness

The restaurant won a reputation for fine service since the wait staff responded to their clients' requests with *alacrity*.

Synonyms: eagerness, swiftness

**VICISSITUDE**

noun (vih sih tood)

## ALLEVIATE

verb (uh <u>lee</u> vee ayt)

to annoy, irritate; puzzle, confuse

The old man who loved his peace and quiet was *vexed* by his neighbor's loud music.

Synonyms: annoy; bother; chafe; exasperate; irk; nettle; peeve; provoke

to ease, to make more bearable

Taking aspirin helps to *alleviate* a headache.

Synonyms: lessen; lighten; mitigate; relieve

**VEX**

verb (vehks)

# AMALGAMATION

noun (uh maal guh may shun)

trace, remnant

*Vestiges* of the former tenant still remained in the apartment, though he hadn't lived there for years.

Synonyms: relic; remains; sign

a merger, a uniting of elements

The *amalgamation* of the two giant companies worried the small mom and pop stores.

Synonyms: compound; fusing

**VESTIGE**

noun (veh stihj)

## AMBIGUOUS

adj (aam bihg yoo uhs)

related to spring; fresh

Bea basked in the balmy *vernal* breezes, happy that winter was coming to an end.

Synonyms: springlike; youthful

doubtful or uncertain; can be interpreted several ways

The directions he gave were so *ambiguous* that we disagreed on which way to turn.

Synonyms: obscure; unclear; vague

**VERNAL**

adj (vuhr nuhl)

**AMELIORATE**

verb (uh meel yuhr ayt)

green with vegetation; inexperienced

He wandered deep into the *verdant* woods in search of mushrooms and other edible flora.

Synonyms: grassy; leafy; wooded

to make better; to improve

The doctor was able to *ameliorate* the patient's suffering using painkillers.

Synonyms: pacify; upgrade; make more tolerable

**VERDANT**

adj (vuhr dnt)

# AMORTIZE

verb (uh mohr tiez)

worldy

The professor's answer was so *verbose* that his student forgot what the original question had been.

Synonyms: longwinded; loquacious; prolix; superfluous

to diminish by installment payments

While college students are notorious for accumulating credit card debt, they are not as well known for *amortizing* it.

**VERBOSE**

adj (vuhr bohs)

## AMULET

noun (aam yoo liht)

filled with truth and accuracy

She had a reputation for *veracity*, so everyone trusted her description of events.

Synonyms: candor; exactitude; fidelity; probity

ornament worn as a charm against evil spirits

Though she claimed it was not because of superstition, Vivian always wore an *amulet* around her neck.

Synonyms: fetish; talisman

**VERACITY**

noun (vuhr aa sih tee)

## ANACHRONISM

noun (uh naak ruh nih suhm)

to respect deeply

In a traditional Confucian society, the young *venerate* their elders, deferring to their elders' wisdom and experience.

Synonyms: adore; honor; idolize; revere

something out of place in time

The aging hippie used *anachronistic* phrases like 'groovy' and 'far out' that had not been popular for years.

Synonyms: archaism; incongruity

**VENERATE**

verb (vehn uhr ayt)

## ANALGESIA

noun (aah nuhl <u>jee</u> zhuh)

respected because of age

All of the villagers sought the *venerable* woman's advice whenever they had a problem.

Synonyms: distinguished; elderly; respectable

a lessening of pain without loss of consciousness

After having her appendix removed, Tatiana welcomed the *analgesia* that the painkillers provided.

**VENERABLE**

adj (veh nehr uh buhl)

## ANALOGOUS

adj (uh <u>naal</u> uh guhs)

varied; marked with different colors

The *variegated* foliage of the jungle allows it to support thousands of animal species.

Synonym: diversified

similar or alike in some way; equivalent to

His mother argued that not going to college was *analogous* to throwing his life away.

Synonyms: alike; comparable; parallel; similar

**VARIEGATED**

adj (vaar ee uh gayt ehd)

to physically sway, to be indecisive

The customer held up the line as he *vacillated* between chocolate-chip or rocky-road ice cream.

Synonyms: dither; falter; fluctuate; oscillate; waver

# ANODYNE

noun (<u>aah</u> nuh dien)

something that calms or soothes pain

The *anodyne* massage helped remove the knots from the lawyer's tense shoulders.

Synonyms: opiate

**VACILLATE**

verb ($\overline{\text{vaa}}$ sihl ayt)

## ANOMALY

noun (uh <u>nahm</u> uh lee)

the practice of lending money at exorbitant rates

The moneylender was convicted of *usury* when it was discovered that he charged 50 percent interest on all his loans.

Synonym: loan-sharking

deviation from what is normal

> Albino animals may display too great an *anomaly* in their coloring to attract normally colored mates.

Synonyms: aberration; abnormality; deviation; irregularity

**USURY**

noun (yoo zhuh ree)

## ANTAGONIZE

verb (aan taa guh niez)

to scold sharply

The teacher *upbraided* the student for scrawling graffiti all over the walls of the school.

Synonyms: berate; chide; rebuke; reproach; tax

to annoy or provoke to anger

The child discovered that he could *antagonize* the cat by pulling its tail.

Synonyms: clash; conflict; incite; irritate; oppose; pester; provoke; vex

**UPBRAID**

verb (uhp brayd)

## ANTIPATHY

noun (aan tih puh thee)

absolute, certain

The jury's verdict was *unequivocal:* the organized crime boss would be locked up for life.

Synonyms: categorical; clear; explicit; express; unambiguous

extreme dislike

The *antipathy* between fans of the rival soccer teams made the game even more electrifying to watch.

Synonyms: animosity; animus; antagonism; aversion; enmity

**UNEQUIVOCAL**

adj (uhn ee kwih vih kuhl)

## APATHY

noun (<u>aa</u> pah thee)

unscrupulous; shockingly unfair or unjust

After she promised me the project, the fact that she gave it to someone else is *unconscionable.*

Synonyms: dishonorable; indefensible

lack of interest or emotion

The *apathy* of voters is so great that fewer than half the people who are eligible to vote actually bother to do so.

Synonyms: disinterest; disregard; indifference; insensibility

**UNCONSCIONABLE**

adj (uhn kahn shuhn uh buhl)

## APOCRYPHAL

adj (uh pahk ruh fuhl)

offense, resentment

The businessman took *umbrage* at the security guard's accusation that he had shoplifted a packet of gum.

Synonyms: asperity; dudgeon; ire; pique; rancor

of questionable authority or authenticity

There is no hard or authoritative evidence to support the *apocryphal* tales that link the Roswell, New Mexico incident to a downed U.F.O.

Synonyms: disputed; doubtful; fictitious; fraudulent

**UMBRAGE**

noun (uhm brihj)

**APOSTATE**

noun (uh pahs tayt)

beginner, novice

An obvious *tyro* at salsa, Millicent received no invitations to dance.

Synonyms: apprentice; fledgling; greenhorn; neophyte; tenderfoot

one who renounces a religious faith

So that he could divorce his wife, the king scoffed at the church doctrines and declared himself an *apostate*.

Synonyms: defector; deserter; traitor

**TYRO**

noun (tie roh)

## APPROBATION

noun (aa pruh <u>bay</u> shuhn)

swollen as from a fluid, bloated

In the process of osmosis, water passes through the walls of *turgid* cells, ensuring that they never contain too much water.

Synonym: distended

approval and praise

> The *approbation* that comedian Jerry Lewis received in France included a medal from the Ministry of Culture.

Synonyms: acclaim; adulation; applause; commendation; compliments

**TURGID**

adj (tuhr jihd)

## ARBITRARY

adj (ahr bih trayr ee)

acute, sharp, incisive; forceful, effective

Tyrone's *trenchant* observations in class made him the professor's favorite student.

Synonyms: biting; caustic; cutting; keen

determined by chance or impulse

> When you lack the information to judge what to do next, you are forced to make an *arbitrary* decision.

Synonyms: changeable; erratic; indiscriminate; random; wayward

**TRENCHANT**

adj (trehn chuhnt)

temporary, lasting a brief time

The reporter lived in *transitory* lodgings, staying in one place only long enough to cover the current story.

Synonyms: ephemeral; evanescent; fleeting; impermanent; momentary

## ARBITRATE

verb (ahr bih trayt)

to judge a dispute between two opposing parties

Since the couple could not come to an agreement, a judge was forced to *arbitrate* their divorce proceedings.

Synonyms: adjudge; adjudicate; determine; intermediate; intervene; judge; moderate; referee; rule

**TRANSITORY**

adj (trahn sih tohr ee)

## ARCHAIC

adj (ahr <u>kay</u> ihk)

---

extreme mental and physical sluggishness

After surgery, the patient's *torpor* lasted several hours until the anesthesia wore off.

Synonyms: apathy; languor

ancient, old-fashioned

Her *archaic* Commodore computer could not run the latest software.

Synonyms: obsolete; outdated; vintage

**TORPOR**

noun (tohr puhr)

## ARDOR

noun (<u>ahr</u> duhr)

a book (usually large and academic)

The teacher was forced to refer to various *tomes* to find the answer to the advanced student's question.

Synonyms: codex; volume

intense and passionate feeling

Bishop's *ardor* for landscape was evident when he passionately described the beauty of the scenic Hudson Valley.

Synonyms: devotion; enthusiasm; fervency; fervidity; fervidness; fervor; fire; passion; zeal; zealousness

**TOME**

noun (tohm)

## ARROGATE

verb (<u>aa</u> ruh gayt)

one who flatters in the hope of gaining favors

The king was surrounded by *toadies* who rushed to agree with whatever outrageous thing he said.

Synonyms: parasite; sycophant

to claim without justification; to claim for oneself without right

Gretchen watched in astonishment as her boss *arrogated* the credit for her brilliant work on the project.

Synonyms: appropriate; presume; take

**TOADY**

noun (toh dee)

## ARTICULATE

adj (ahr tih kyuh luht)

long, harsh speech or verbal attack

Observers were shocked at the manager's *tirade* over such a minor mistake.

Synonyms: diatribe; fulmination; harangue; obloquy; revilement; vilification

able to speak clearly and expressively

She is extremely *articulate* when it comes to expressing her pro-labor views; as a result, unions are among her strongest supporters.

Synonyms: eloquent; expressive; fluent; lucid; silver-tongued; smooth-spoken

**TIRADE**

noun (tīe rayd)

## ASSAIL

verb (uh sayl)

earthly; down-to-earth, commonplace

Many "extraterrestrial" objects turn out to be *terrestrial* in origin, as when flying saucers turn out to be normal airplanes.

Synonyms: earthbound; mundane; sublunary; tellurian; terrene

to attack, assault

The foreign army will try to *assail* our bases, but they will not be successful in their attack.

Synonyms: beset; strike; storm

**TERRESTRIAL**

adj (tuh reh stree uhl)

## ASSUAGE

verb (uh swayj) (uh swayzh) (uh swahzh)

gaudy, cheap, showy

The performer changed into her *tawdry*, spangled costume and stepped out onto the stage to do her show.

Synonyms: flashy; loud; meretricious

to make something unpleasant less severe

Like many people, Philip used food to *assuage* his sense of loneliness.

Synonyms: allay; alleviate; appease; ease; lighten; mitigate; mollify; pacify

**TAWDRY**

adj (taw dree)

# ATTENUATE

verb (uh tehn yoo ayt)

digressing, diverting

Your argument is interesting, but it's *tangential* to the matter at hand, so I suggest we get back to the point.

Synonyms: digressive; extraneous; inconsequential; irrelevant; peripheral

to reduce in force or degree; to weaken

The Bill of Rights *attenuated* the traditional power of government to change laws at will.

Synonyms: debilitate; devitalize; dilute; enervate; enfeeble; rarefy; sap; thin; undermine; undo; unnerve; water; weaken

**TANGENTIAL**

*adj* (taan jehn shuhl)

## AUDACIOUS

adj (aw <u>day</u> shuhs)

claw of an animal, especially a bird of prey

A vulture holds its prey in its *talons* while it dismembers it with its beak.

Synonyms: claw; nail

fearless and daring

The *audacious* peasant dared to insult the king's mother.

Synonyms: adventuresome; assertive; bold; brave; courageous; daring

**TALON**

noun (taa luhn)

## AUGURY

noun (aw gyuh ree) (aw guh ree)

silent, not talkative

The clerk's *taciturn* nature earned him the nickname Silent Bob.

Synonyms: laconic; reticent

prophecy; prediction of events

Troy hoped the rainbow was an *augury* of good things to come.

Synonyms: auspices; harbinger; omen; portent; presage

---

**TACITURN**

adj (taa sih tuhrn)

**AUGUST**

adj (aw <u>guhst</u>)

done without using words

Although not a word was said, everyone in the room knew that a *tacit* agreement had been made about what course of action to take.

Synonyms: implicit; implied; undeclared; unsaid; unuttered

dignified, grandiose

The *august* view of the Grand Teton summit took my breath away.

Synonyms: admirable; awesome; grand; majestic

**TACIT**

adj (taa siht)

**AUSTERE**

adj (aw steer)

temporary irregularity in musical rhythm

A jazz enthusiast will appreciate the use of *syncopation* in this musical genre.

severe or stern in appearance; undecorated

The lack of decoration makes Zen temples seem *austere* to the untrained eye.

Synonyms: bleak; dour; grim; hard; harsh; severe

**SYNCOPATION**

noun (sihn cuh pay shun)

cooperation, mutual helpfulness

The rhino and the tick-eating bird live in *symbiosis*; the rhino gives the bird food in the form of ticks, and the bird rids the rhino of parasites.

Synonyms: association; interdependence

## AXIOM

noun (aak see uhm)

premise; postulate; self-evident truth

Halle lived her life based on the *axioms* her grandmother had passed on to her.

Synonyms: adage; apothegm; aphorism; maxim; rule

**SYMBIOSIS**

noun (sihm bee ōh sihs)

# BANAL

adj (buh naal) (bay nuhl) (buh nahl)

a self-serving flatterer, yes-man

Dreading criticism, the actor surrounded himself with admirers and *sycophants.*

Synonyms: bootlicker; fawner; lickspittle; toady

predictable; clichéd, boring

> His conversation consisted of *banal* phrases like ‘Have a nice day’ or ‘Another day, another dollar.’

Synonyms: bland; clichéd; commonplace; tired; trite; vapid; worn-out

**SYCOPHANT**

noun (sih kuh fuhnt)

## BELFRY

noun (behl free)

a person devoted to pleasure and luxury

A confirmed *sybarite*, the nobleman fainted at the thought of having to leave his palace and live in a small cottage.

Synonyms: hedonist; pleasuremonger; sensualist

bell tower; room in which a bell is hung

The town was shocked when a bag of money was found stashed in the old *belfry* of the church.

Synonyms: spire; steeple

**SYBARITE**

noun (sih buh riet)

## BEVY

noun (beh vee)

rude and bad-tempered

When asked to clean the windshield, the *surly* gas station attendant tossed a dirty rag at the customer and walked away.

Synonyms: gruff; grumpy; testy

group

As predicted, a *bevy* of teenagers surrounded the rock star's limousine.

Synonyms: band; bunch; gang; pack; troop

**SURLY**

adj (suhr lee)

excessive amount

Because of the *surfeit* of pigs, pork prices have never been lower.

Synonyms: glut; plethora; repletion; superfluity; surplus

## BIFURCATE

verb (bi fuhr kayt) (bi fuhr kayt)

divide into two parts

> The large corporation just released a press statement announcing its plans to *bifurcate*.

Synonym: bisect

**SURFEIT**

noun (suhr fiht)

## BILK

verb (bihlk)

to replace (another) by force; to take the place of

The overthrow of the government meant a new leader to *supplant* the tyrannical former one.

Synonyms: displace; supersede

to cheat, defraud

> When the greedy salesman realized that his customer spoke poor French, he *bilked* the tourist out of 20 euros.

Synonyms: beat; defraud; diddle; gyp; overreach

**SUPPLANT**

verb (suh plaant)

## BLIGHT

verb (bliet)

to tarnish, taint

With the help of a public relations firm, he was able to restore his *sullied* reputation.

Synonyms: besmirch; defile

to afflict; to destroy

The farmers feared that the night's frost would *blight* the potato crops entirely.

Synonyms: damage; plague

**SULLY**

verb (suh lee)

## BLITHE

adj (blieth)

lofty or grand

The music was so *sublime* that it transformed the rude surroundings into a special place.

Synonyms: august; exalted; glorious; grand; magnificent; majestic; noble; resplendent; superb

joyful, cheerful, or without appropriate thought

Summer finally came, and the *blithe* students spent their days at the beach.

Synonyms: carefree; lighthearted; merry

**SUBLIME**

adj (suh bliem)

## BOLSTER

verb (<u>bohl</u> stuhr)

trick designed to deceive an enemy

The Trojan Horse must be one of the most successful military *stratagems* used throughout history.

Synonyms: artifice; feint; maneuver; ruse; wile

to support; to prop up

The presence of giant footprints *bolstered* the argument that Bigfoot was in the area.

Synonyms: brace; buttress; crutch; prop; stay; support; sustain; underpinning; uphold

**STRATAGEM**

noun (straa tuh juhm)

# BOMBASTIC

adj (bahm <u>baast</u> ihk)

unemotional, lacking sensitivity

The prisoner appeared *stolid* and unaffected by the judge's harsh sentence.

Synonyms: apathetic; impassive; indifferent; phlegmatic; stoical; unconcerned

pompous in speech and manner

Mussolini's speeches were mostly *bombastic*; his boasting and outrageous claims had no basis in fact.

Synonyms: bloated; declamatory; fustian; grandiloquent; grandiose; high-flown; magniloquent; orotund; pretentious; rhetorical; self-important

**STOLID**

adj (stah lihd)

## BONHOMIE

noun (bah nuh <u>mee</u>)

a mark of shame or discredit

In *The Scarlet Letter* Hester Prynne was required to wear the letter 'A' on her clothes as a public *stigma* for her adultery.

Synonyms: blemish; blot; opprobrium; stain; taint

good-natured geniality; atmosphere of good cheer

The aspects of her job that Dana loved the most were the flexible hours and the pleasant *bonhomie* in the office.

**STIGMA**

noun (stihg mah)

**BOOR**

noun (bohr)

extremely loud

Cullen couldn't hear her speaking over the *stentorian* din of the game on TV.

Synonyms: clamorous; noisy

crude person, one lacking manners or taste

"That utter *boor* ruined my recital with his constant guffawing!" wailed the pianist.

Synonyms: clod; lout; oaf; vulgarian; yahoo

**STENTORIAN**

adj (stehn tohr ee yehn)

## BURGEON

verb (buhr juhn)

a state of static balance or equilibrium; stagnation

The rusty, ivy-covered World War II tank had obviously been in *stasis* for years.

Synonyms: inertia; standstill

to grow and flourish

Faulkner neither confirmed nor denied stories about himself, allowing rumor to *burgeon* where it would.

Synonyms: bloom; burgeon; flourish; prosper; thrive

**STASIS**

noun (stay sihs)

## BURNISH

verb (buhr nihsh)

frolicsome, playful

The lakeside vacation meant more *sportive* opportunities for the kids than the wine tour through France.

Synonyms: frisky; merry

to polish

He *burnished* the silver coffee pot until it shone brightly.

Synonyms: buff; luster; polish; scour

**SPORTIVE**

adj (spohr tihv)

## CABAL

noun (kuh <u>bahl</u>)

deceptively attractive; seemingly plausible but fallacious

The student's *specious* excuse for being late sounded legitimate, but was proved otherwise when his teacher called his home.

Synonyms: illusory; ostensible; plausible; sophistic; spurious

a secret group seeking to overturn something

The boys on the street formed a *cabal* to keep girls out of their tree house.

Synonyms: camp; circle; clan; clique; coterie; in-group; mafia; mob; ring

**SPECIOUS**

adj (spee shuhs)

**CACOPHONY**

noun (kuh <u>kah</u> fuh nee)

highly self-disciplined; frugal, austere

When he was in training, the athlete preferred to live in a *spartan* room so he could shut out all distractions.

Synonyms: restrained; simple

harsh, jarring noise

The junior high orchestra created an almost unbearable *cacophony* as they tried to tune their instruments.

Synonyms: chaos; clamor; din; discord; disharmony; noise

**SPARTAN**

adj (spahr tihn)

## CALUMNY

noun (<u>kaa</u> luhm nee)

causing sleep or lethargy

The movie proved to be so *soporific* that soon loud snores were heard throughout the cinema.

Synonyms: hypnotic; narcotic; slumberous; somnolent

a false and malicious accusation; misrepresentation

The unscrupulous politician used *calumny* to bring down his opponent in the senatorial race.

Synonyms: defamation; libel; slander

**SOPORIFIC**

adj (sahp uhr ihf ihk)

**CANARD**

noun (kuh nard)

grammatical mistake; blunder in speech

"I ain't going with you," she said, obviously unaware of her *solecism*.

Synonyms: blooper; faux pas; vulgarism

a lie

That tabloid's feature story about a goat giving birth to a human child was clearly a *canard*.

Synonyms: falsehood; falsity; fib; misrepresentation; prevarication; tale; untruth

**SOLECISM**

noun (sah lih sishz uhm)

**CANDID**

adj (<u>kaan</u> did)

nickname

One of Ronald Reagan's *sobriquets* was "The Gipper."

Synonyms: alias; pseudonym

impartial and honest in speech

The observations of a child can be charming since they are *candid* and unpretentious.

Synonyms: direct; forthright; frank; honest; open; sincere; straight; straightforward; undisguised

**SOBRIQUET**

noun (soh brih keht)

## CAPRICIOUS

adj (kuh <u>pree</u> shuhs) (kuh <u>prih</u> shuhs)

to calm down or moderate

In order to *slake* his curiosity, Bryan finally took a tour backstage at the theater.

Synonyms: moderate; quench; satisfy

changing one's mind quickly and often

Queen Elizabeth I was quite *capricious*; her courtiers could never be sure which one would catch her fancy.

Synonyms: arbitrary; chance; changeable; erratic; fickle; inconstant; mercurial; random; whimsical; willful

**SLAKE**

verb (slayk)

## CARTOGRAPHY

noun (kahr tahg ruh fee)

a well-paying job or office that requires little or no work

The corrupt mayor made sure to set up all his relatives in *sinecures* within the administration.

science or art of making maps

> Gail's interest in *cartography* may stem from the extensive traveling she did as a child.

Synonyms: charting; surveying; topography

**SINECURE**

noun (sien ih kyoor)

## CASTIGATE

verb (<u>kaa</u> stih gayt)

angelic, sweet

Selena's *seraphic* appearance belied her nasty, bitter personality.

Synonyms: cherubic; heavenly

to punish or criticize harshly

Martina *castigated* her boyfriend for not remembering her birthday.

Synonyms: admonish; chastise; chide; rebuke; reprimand; reproach; reprove; scold; tax; upbraid

**SERAPHIC**

adj (seh rah fihk)

# CATALYST

noun (kaa tuh lihst)

aware; conscious, able to perceive

The anesthetic didn't work, and I was still *sentient* when the dentist started drilling!

Synonyms: feeling; intelligent; thinking

something that brings about a change in something else

> The imposition of harsh taxes was the *catalyst* that finally brought on the revolution.

Synonyms: accelerator; impetus; stimulant

**SENTIENT**

adj (sehn shuhnt)

## CATHOLIC

adj (<u>kaa</u> thuh lihk) (<u>kaa</u> thlihk)

behavior that promotes rebellion or civil disorder against the state

Li was arrested for *sedition* after he gave a fiery speech in the main square.

Synonyms: conspiracy; insurrection

universal; broad and comprehensive

Hot tea with honey is a *catholic* remedy for a sore throat.

Synonyms: extensive; general

**SEDITION**

noun (sih dih shuhn)

## CAUSTIC

adj (kah stihk)

trace amount

This poison is so powerful that no more than a *scintilla* of it is needed to kill a horse.

Synonyms: atom; iota; mote; spark; speck

biting in wit

> Dorothy Parker gained her reputation for being *caustic* from her cutting, yet witty, insults.

Synonyms: acerbic; biting; mordant; trenchant

**SCINTILLA**

noun (sihn tihl uh)

## CHAOS

noun (kay ahs)

to satisfy fully or overindulge

His desire for power was so great that nothing less than complete control of the country could *satiate* it.

Synonyms: cloy; glut; gorge; surfeit

great disorder or confused situation

In most religious traditions, God created an ordered universe from *chaos*.

Synonyms: clutter; confusion; disarrangement; disarray; disorder; disorderliness; disorganization; jumble; mess; muddle; scramble; snarl; topsy-turviness; turmoil

**SATIATE**

verb (say shee ayt)

## CHAUVINIST

noun (shoh vuh nist)

cynical; scornfully mocking

Isabella was offended by the *sardonic* way in which her date made fun of her ideas and opinions.

Synonyms: acerbic; caustic; sarcastic; satirical; snide

someone prejudiced in favor of a group to which he or she belongs

> The attitude that men should earn more money than women is common among male *chauvinists.*

Synonyms: biased; colored; one-sided; partial; partisan; prejudicial

**SARDONIC**

adj (sahr dah nihk)

**CHICANERY**

noun (shih <u>kayn</u> ree) (shi <u>kay</u> nuh ree)

ruddy; cheerfully optimistic

A *sanguine* person thinks the glass is half full, whereas a depressed person thinks it's half empty.

Synonyms: confident; hopeful; positive; rosy; rubicund

deception by means of craft or guile

Dishonest used-car salesmen often use *chicanery* to sell their beat-up old cars.

Synonyms: artifice; conniving; craftiness; deception; deviousness; misrepresentation

**SANGUINE**

adj (saan gwuhn)

**CIRCUMSPECT**

adj (suhr kuhm spehkt)

healthful

Rundown and sickly, Rita hoped that the fresh mountain air would have a *salubrious* effect on her health.

Synonyms: bracing; curative; medicinal; therapeutic; tonic

cautious, aware of potential consequences

She was *circumspect* in her language and behavior when introduced to her fiancee's parents.

Synonyms: alert; cautious; heedful; mindful; prudent; solicitous; vigilant; wary

**SALUBRIOUS**

adj (suh $\overline{\text{loo}}$ bree uhs)

## CLOYING

adj (<u>kloy</u> ing)

prominent, of notable significance

His most *salient* characteristic is his tendency to dominate every conversation.

Synonyms: marked; noticeable; outstanding

sickly sweet; excessive

When Enid and Jay first started dating, their *cloying* affection toward one another often made their friends ill.

Synonyms: excessive; fulsome

**SALIENT**

adj (say lee uhnt)

## COALESCE

verb (koh uh lehs)

shrewd, wise

Owls have a reputation for being *sagacious*, perhaps because of their big eyes, which resemble glasses.

Synonyms: astute; judicious; perspicacious; sage; wise

to grow together to form a single whole

The sun and planets eventually *coalesced* out of a vast cloud of gas and dust.

Synonyms: amalgamate; blend; coalesce; condense; consolidate; fuse; unite

**SAGACIOUS**

adj (suh gay shuhs)

**COFFER**

noun (<u>kah</u> fuhr)

extremely sacred; beyond criticism

Many people considered Mother Teresa to be *sacrosanct* and would not tolerate any criticism of her.

Synonyms: holy; inviolable; off-limits

strongbox; large chest for money

The bulletproof glass of the *coffer* is what keeps the crown jewels secure.

Synonyms: chest; exchequer; treasury; war chest

**SACROSANCT**

adj (saa kroh saankt)

## COGENT

adj (koh juhnt)

rural

The *rustic* cabin was an ideal setting for a vacation in the country.

Synonyms: bucolic; pastoral

convincing and well-reasoned

Swayed by the *cogent* argument of the defense, the jury had no choice but to acquit the defendant.

Synonyms: convincing; persuasive; solid; sound; telling; valid

**RUSTIC**

adj (ruh stihk)

very highly ornamented; relating to an 18$^{th}$ century artistic style of elaborate ornamentation

The ornate furniture in the house reminded Tatiana of the *rococo* style.

Synonyms: intricate; ornate

# COLLUSION

noun (kuh loo zhuhn)

collaboration, complicity, conspiracy

It came to light that the police chief and the mafia had a *collusion* in running the numbers racket.

Synonyms: connivance; intrigue; machination

**ROCOCO**

adj (ruh koh koh) (roh kuh koh)

## CONDONE

verb (kuhn <u>dohn</u>)

humorous in a vulgar way

The court jester's *ribald* brand of humor delighted the rather uncouth king.

Synonyms: coarse; gross; indelicate; lewd; obscene

to overlook, to pardon, to disregard

Some theorists believe that failing to prosecute minor crimes is the same as *condoning* an air of lawlessness.

Synonyms: exculpate; excuse; pardon; remit

**RIBALD**

adj (rih buhld)

## CONNOISSEUR

noun (kah nuh suhr)

effective writing or speaking

Lincoln's talent for *rhetoric* was evident in his beautifully expressed Gettysburg Address.

Synonyms: eloquence; oratory

a person with expert knowledge or discriminating tastes

Dr. Crane was a *connoisseur* of fine food and wine, drinking and eating only the best.

Synonyms: authority; epicure; expert; gastronome; gourmet

**RHETORIC**

noun (reh tuhr ihk)

## CONTRITE

adj (kuhn <u>triet</u>)

silent, reserved

Physically small and verbally *reticent*, Joan Didion often went unnoticed by those she was reporting upon.

Synonyms: cool; introverted; laconic; standoffish; taciturn; undemonstrative

deeply sorrowful and repentant for a wrong

After three residents were mugged in the lobby while the watchman was away from his post, he felt very *contrite*.

Synonyms: apologetic; regretful; remorseful

**RETICENT**

adj (reh tih suhnt)

impatient; uneasy, restless

The passengers became *restive* after having to wait in line for hours and began to shout complaints at the airline staff.

Synonyms: agitated; anxious; fretful

## CONTUMACIOUS

adj (kahn tuh <u>may</u> shuhs)

rebellious

The *contumacious* teenager ran away from home when her parents told her she was grounded.

Synonyms: factious; insubordinate; insurgent; mutinous; rebellious; seditious

**RESTIVE**

adj (reh stihv)

## CONVOLUTED

adj (kahn vuh <u>loo</u> tehd)

to return or repay

Thanks for offering to lend me $1,000, but I know I'll never be able to *requite* your generosity.

Synonyms: compensate; reciprocate

intricate and complicated

> Although many people bought the professor's book, few people could follow its *convoluted* ideas and theories.

Synonyms: Byzantine; complex; elaborate; intricate; knotty; labyrinthine; perplexing; tangled

**REQUITE**

verb (rih kwiet)

## CORROBORATE

verb (kuh rahb uhr ayt)

to reject the validity of

The old woman's claim that she was Russian royalty was *repudiated* when DNA tests showed she was of no relation to them.

Synonyms: deny; disavow; disclaim; disown; renounce

to support with evidence

All the DA needed was fingerprints to *corroborate* the witness's testimony.

Synonyms: authenticate; back; buttress; confirm; substantiate; validate; verify

**REPUDIATE**

verb (ree pyoo dee ayt)

## COSSET

verb (<u>kah</u> suht)

relaxation, leisure

After working hard every day in the busy city, Mike finds his *repose* on weekends playing golf with friends.

Synonyms: calmness; tranquility

to pamper, to treat with great care

Marta just loves to *cosset* her first and only grandchild.

Synonyms: cater to; cuddle; dandle; fondle; love; pamper; pet; spoil

**REPOSE**

noun (rih pōhz)

## COTERIE

noun (koh tuh ree) (koh tuh ree)

abundantly supplied, complete

The gigantic supermarket was *replete* with consumer products of every kind.

Synonyms: abounding; full

an intimate group of persons with a similar purpose

Angel invited a *coterie* of fellow stamp enthusiasts to a stamp-trading party.

Synonyms: clique; set

**REPLETE**

adj (rih pleet)

**CRAVEN**

adj (<u>kray</u> vuhn)

meal or mealtime

Ravi prepared a delicious *repast* of chicken tikka and naan.

Synonyms: banquet; feast

lacking courage

The *craven* lion cringed in the corner of his cage, terrified of the mouse.

Synonyms: faint-hearted; spineless; timid

**REPAST**

noun (rih paast)

## CREDULOUS

adj (<u>kreh</u> juh luhs)

response

Patrick tried desperately to think of a clever *rejoinder* to Marianna's joke, but he couldn't.

Synonyms: retort; riposte

too trusting; gullible

Though many 4-year-olds believe in the Tooth Fairy, only the most *credulous* 9-year-olds also believe in her.

Synonyms: naïve; susceptible; trusting

**REJOINDER**

noun (rih joyn duhr)

## CRESCENDO

noun (kruh shehn doh)

relief from wrong or injury

Seeking *redress* for the injuries she had received in the accident, Doreen sued the driver of the truck that had hit her.

Synonyms: amends; indemnity; quittance; reparation; restitution

steadily increasing in volume or force

> The *crescendo* of tension became unbearable as Evel Knievel prepared to jump his motorcycle over the school buses.

Synonyms: acme; capstone; climax; crest; culmen; culmination; meridian; peak

**REDRESS**

noun (rih drehs)

## CUPIDITY

noun (kyoo pih dih tee)

to make thinner or sparser

Since the atmosphere *rarefies* as altitudes increase, the air at the top of very tall mountains is too thin to breathe.

Synonyms: attenuate; thin

greed; strong desire

The thief stared at the shining jewels with *cupidity* in his gleaming eyes.

Synonyms: avarice; covetousness; rapacity

**RAREFY**

verb (rayr uh fie)

## CURMUDGEON

noun (kuhr muh juhn)

witty, skillful storyteller

The *raconteur* kept all the passengers entertained with his stories during the six-hour flight.

Synonyms: anecdotalist; monologist

cranky person, usually old

Ernesto was a notorious *curmudgeon* who snapped at anyone who disturbed him.

**RACONTEUR**

noun (raa cahn tuhr)

## DEBUTANTE

noun (<u>dehb</u> yoo tahnt)

occurring daily; commonplace

The sight of people singing on the street is so *quotidian* in New York that passersby rarely react to it.

Synonyms: everyday; normal; usual

young woman making debut in high society

The *debutante* spent hours dressing for her very first ball, hoping to catch the eye of an eligible bachelor.

Synonyms: lady; maiden

**QUOTIDIAN**

adj (kwo tih dee uhn)

## DECLIVITY

noun (dih klih vih tee)

overly idealistic, impractical

The practical Danuta was skeptical of her roommate's *quixotic* plans to build a roller coaster in their yard.

Synonyms: capricious; impulsive; romantic; unrealistic

downward slope

Because the village was situated on the *declivity* of a hill, it never flooded.

Synonyms: decline; descent; grade; slant; tilt

**QUIXOTIC**

adj (kwihk sah tihk)

## DECOROUS

adj (<u>deh</u> kuhr uhs) (deh <u>kohr</u> uhs)

motionless

Many animals are *quiescent* over the winter months, minimizing activity in order to conserve energy.

Synonyms: dormant; latent

proper, tasteful, socially correct

The countess trained her daughters in the finer points of *decorous* behavior, hoping they would make a good impression when she presented them at Court.

Synonyms: appropriate; courteous; polite

**QUIESCENT**

adj (kwie $\overline{\text{eh}}$ sihnt)

## DECORUM

noun (deh kohr uhm)

inclined to complain, irritable

Curtis's complaint letter received prompt attention after the company labeled him a *querulous* potential troublemaker.

Synonyms: peevish; puling; sniveling; whiny

appropriateness of behavior or conduct; propriety

The countess complained that the vulgar peasants lacked the *decorum* appropriate for a visit to the palace.

Synonyms: correctness; decency; etiquette; manners; mores; propriety; seemliness

**QUERULOUS**

adj (kwehr yoo luhs)

**DEFACE**

verb (dih <u>fays</u>)

cowardly, without courage

The *pusillanimous* man would not enter the yard where the miniature poodle was barking.

Synonyms: cowardly; timid

to mar the appearance of, to vandalize

After the wall was torn down, the students began to *deface* the statues of Communist leaders of the former Eastern bloc.

Synonyms: disfigure; impair; spoil

**PUSILLANIMOUS**

adj (pyoo suh laa nih muhs)

# DEFERENCE

noun (<u>deh</u> fuh ruhn(t)s) (<u>def</u> ruhn(t)s)

sharp and irritating to the senses

The smoke from the burning tires was extremely *pungent.*

Synonyms: acrid; caustic; piquant; poignant; stinging

respect, courtesy

The respectful young law clerk treated the Supreme Court justice with the utmost *deference*.

Synonyms: courtesy; homage; honor; obeisance; respect; reverence; veneration

**PUNGENT**

adj (puhn juhnt)

**DELETERIOUS**

adj (dehl ih <u>teer</u> ee uhs)

beauty

The mortals gazed in admiration at Venus, stunned by her incredible *pulchritude*.

Synonyms: comeliness; gorgeousness; handsomeness; loveliness; prettiness

subtly or unexpectedly harmful

> If only we had known the clocks were defective before putting them on the market, it wouldn't have been quite so *deleterious* to our reputation.

Synonyms: adverse; inimical; injurious; hurtful

**PULCHRITUDE**

noun (puhl kruh tood)

## DEMAGOGUE

noun (deh muh gahg) (deh muh gawg)

boxing

*Pugilism* has been defended as a positive outlet for aggressive impulses.

Synonyms: fighting; sparring

a leader, rabble-rouser, usually appealing to emotion or prejudice

He began his career as a *demagogue*, giving fiery speeches at political rallies.

Synonyms: agitator; inciter; instigator

**PUGILISM**

noun (pyoo juhl ih suhm)

## DEMUR

verb (dih <u>muhr</u>)

childish, immature, silly

Olivia's boyfriend's *puerile* antics are really annoying; sometimes he acts like a five-year-old!

Synonyms: infantile; jejune; juvenile

to express doubts or objections

When scientific authorities claimed that all the planets revolved around the Earth, Galileo, with his superior understanding of the situation, was forced to *demur*.

Synonyms: dissent; expostulate; kick; protest; remonstrate

**PUERILE**

adj (pyoo ruhl)

## DERIDE

verb (dih <u>ried</u>)

wisdom, caution or restraint

The college student exhibited *prudence* by obtaining practical experience along with her studies, which greatly strengthened her résumé.

Synonyms: astuteness; circumspection; discretion; frugality; judiciousness; providence; thrift

to speak of or treat with contempt, to mock

The awkward child was often *derided* by his 'cooler' peers.

Synonyms: gibe; jeer; mock; ridicule

**PRUDENCE**

noun (proo dehns)

## DESICCATE

verb (<u>deh</u> sih kayt)

the quality of behaving in a proper manner, obeying rules and customs

The aristocracy maintained a high level of *propriety*, adhering to even the most minor social rules.

Synonyms: appropriateness; decency; decorum; modesty

to dry out thoroughly

After a few weeks lying in the desert, the cow's carcass became completely *desiccated*.

Synonyms: dehydrate; dry; parch

**PROPRIETY**

noun (pruh prie uh tee)

## DESULTORY

adj (dehs uhl tohr ee) (dehz uhl tohr ee)

to conciliate, to appease

Because their gods were angry and vengeful, the Vikings *propitiated* them with many sacrifices.

Synonyms: appease; conciliate; mollify; pacify; placate

jumping from one thing to another; disconnected

> Athena had a *desultory* academic record; she had changed majors 12 times in three years.

Synonyms: erratic; haphazard; indiscriminate; random

**PROPITIATE**

verb (proh pih shee ayt)

to increase in number quickly

Although he only kept two guinea pigs initially, they *proliferated* to such an extent that he soon had dozens.

Synonyms: breed; multiply; procreate; propagate; reproduce; spawn

## DIAPHANOUS

adj (die <u>aaf</u> uh nuhs)

allowing light to show through; delicate

These *diaphanous* curtains do nothing to block out the sunlight.

Synonyms: gauzy; sheer; tenuous; translucent; transparent

**PROLIFERATE**

verb (proh lih fuhr ayt)

## DIATRIBE

noun (die uh trieb)

corrupt, degenerate

Some historians claim that it was the Romans' decadent, *profligate* behavior that led to the decline of the Roman Empire.

Synonyms: dissolute; extravagant; improvident; prodigal; wasteful

an abusive, condemnatory speech

The trucker bellowed a *diatribe* at the driver who had cut him off.

Synonyms: fulmination; harangue; invective

**PROFLIGATE**

adj (praa flih guht)

## DICTUM

noun (<u>dihk</u> tuhm)

lavish, wasteful

The *prodigal* son quickly wasted all of his inheritance on a lavish lifestyle devoted to pleasure.

Synonyms: extravagant; lavish; profligate; spendthrift; wasteful

authoritative statement

"You have time to lean, you have time to clean," was the *dictum* our boss made us live by.

Synonyms: adage; apothegm; aphorism; decree; edict

**PRODIGAL**

adj (prah dih guhl)

a natural inclination or predisposition

Her childhood love of acting, singing, and adoration indicated a *proclivity* for the theater in later life.

Synonyms: bias; leaning; partiality; penchant; predilection; predisposition; prejudice; propensity

## DIFFIDENT

adj (dih fih dint)

lacking self-confidence

> Steve was *diffident* during the job interview because of his nervous nature and lack of experience in the field.

Synonyms: backward; bashful; coy; demure; modest; retiring; self-effacing; shy; timid

**PROCLIVITY**

noun (proh clih vuh tee)

## DILATE

verb (<u>die</u> layt) (die <u>layt</u>)

complete honesty and integrity

George Washington's reputation for *probity* is illustrated in the legend about his inability to lie after he chopped down the cherry tree.

Synonyms: integrity; morality; rectitude; uprightness; virtue

to make larger, to expand

When you enter a darkened room, the pupils of your eyes *dilate* so as to let in more light.

Synonyms: amplify; develop; elaborate; enlarge; expand; expatiate

**PROBITY**

noun (proh bih tee)

## DILATORY

adj (dihl uh tohr ee)

fresh and clean, uncorrupted

Since concerted measures had been taken to prevent looting, the archeological site was still *pristine* when researchers arrived.

Synonyms: innocent; undamaged

intended to delay, procrastinating

The congressman used *dilatory* measures to delay the passage of the bill.

Synonyms: sluggish; putting off

**PRISTINE**

adj (prih steen)

## DILETTANTE

noun (<u>dih</u> luh tahnt)

to lie or deviate from the truth

Rather than admit that he had overslept again, the employee *prevaricated* and claimed that heavy traffic had prevented him from arriving at work on time.

Synonyms: equivocate; lie; perjure

someone with an amateurish and superficial interest in a topic

Jerry's friends were such *dilettantes* they seemed to have new jobs and hobbies every week.

Synonyms: amateur; dabbler; rookie

**PREVARICATE**

verb (prih vaar uh cayt)

## DIRGE

noun (duhrj)

having foresight

Jonah's decision to sell the apartment seemed to be a *prescient* one, as its value soon dropped by half.

Synonyms: augural; divinatory; mantic; oracular; premonitory

a funeral hymn or mournful speech

Melville wrote the poem "A *Dirge* for James McPherson" for the funeral of a Union general who was killed in 1864.

Synonyms: elegy; lament

**PRESCIENT**

adj (preh shuhnt)

**DISABUSE**

verb (dih suh byuze)

short summary of facts

Fara wrote a *précis* of her thesis on the epic poem to share with the class.

Synonym: summation

to set right, to free from error

> The scientist's observations *disabused* scholars of the notion that wheat could be turned into gold.

Synonyms: correct; dismiss; undeceive

**PRÉCIS**

noun (pray see) (pray see)

**DISCERN**

verb (dihs <u>uhrn</u>)

to throw violently or bring about abruptly; lacking deliberation

Bob and Edna's whirlwind courtship *precipitated* their hasty nuptials.

Synonyms: hurl; rush

to perceive, to recognize

It is easy to *discern* the difference between butter and butter-flavored topping.

Synonyms: differentiate; discriminate; distinguish

**PRECIPITATE**

verb (preh sih puh tayt)

## DISPARATE

adj (dih spuh ruht) (di spar uht)

meaningless, foolish talk

Her husband's mindless *prattle* drove Heidi insane; sometimes she wished he would just shut up.

Synonyms: babble; blather; chatter; drivel; gibberish

fundamentally different; entirely unlike

Although the twins are physically identical, their personalities are *disparate*.

Synonyms: different; dissimilar; divergent; diverse; variant; various

**PRATTLE**

noun (praa tuhl)

## DISSEMBLE

verb (dihs sehm buhl)

practical, as opposed to idealistic

While idealistic gamblers think they can get rich by frequenting casinos, *pragmatic* gamblers realize that the odds are heavily stacked against them.

Synonyms: rational; realistic

to present a false appearance, to disguise one's real intentions or character

The villain could *dissemble* to the police no longer—he admitted the deed and tore up the floor to reveal the stash of stolen money.

Synonyms: camouflage; cloak; feign

**PRAGMATIC**

adj (praag maa tihk)

**DISSONANCE**

noun (dihs uh nuhns)

a monarch or ruler with great power

Alex was much kinder before he assumed the role of *potentate*.

Synonyms: dominator; leader

a harsh and disagreeable combination, especially of sounds

> Cognitive *dissonance* is the inner conflict produced when long-standing beliefs are contradicted by new evidence.

Synonyms: clash; contention; discord; dissension; dissent; dissidence; friction; strife; variance

**POTENTATE**

noun (poh tehn tayt)

## DISTAFF

noun (dis taf)

to assume as real or conceded; propose as an explanation

Before proving the math formula, we needed to *posit* that *x* and *y* were real numbers.

Synonym: suggest

the female branch of a family

The lazy husband refused to cook dinner for his wife, joking that the duty belongs to the *distaff's* side.

**POSIT**

verb (pah siht)

**DISTEND**

verb (dih <u>stehnd</u>)

a speaker of many languages

Ling's extensive travels have helped her to become a true *polyglot*.

to swell, inflate, bloat

Her stomach was *distended* after she gorged on the six-course meal.

Synonyms: broaden; bulge

**POLYGLOT**

noun (pah lee glaht)

## DITHER

verb (dihth uhr)

shrewd and practical in managing or dealing with things; diplomatic

She was wise to curb her tongue and was able to explain her problem to the judge in a respectful and *politic* manner.

Synonym: tactful

to act confusedly or without clear purpose

Ellen *dithered* around her apartment, uncertain how to tackle the family crisis.

Synonyms: falter; hesitate; vacillate; waffle; waver

**POLITIC**

adj (pah lih tihk)

## DIURNAL

adj (die uhr nuhl)

controversy, argument; verbal attack

The candidate's *polemic* against his opponent was vicious and small-minded rather than convincing and well-reasoned.

Synonyms: denunciation; refutation

existing during the day

*Diurnal* creatures tend to become inactive during the night.

Synonyms: daylight; daytime

**POLEMIC**

noun (puh leh mihk)

## DIVINE

verb (dih vien)

courageous, spunky

The *plucky* young nurse dove into the foxhole, determined to help the wounded soldier.

Synonyms: bold; brave; gutsy

to foretell or know by inspiration

The fortune-teller *divined* from the pattern of the tea leaves that her customer would marry five times.

Synonyms: auger; foresee; intuit; predict; presage

**PLUCKY**

adj (pluh kee)

## DOCTRINAIRE

adj (dahk truh nayr)

excess

Assuming that more was better, the defendant offered the judge a *plethora* of excuses.

Synonyms: glut; overabundance; superfluity; surfeit

rigidly devoted to theories without regard for practicality; dogmatic

> The professor's manner of teaching was considered *doctrinaire* for such a liberal school.

Synonyms: dictatorial; inflexible

**PLETHORA**

noun (pleh thor uh)

## DOGMA

noun (<u>dahg</u> muh) (<u>dawg</u> muh)

crude or coarse; characteristic of commoners

After five weeks of rigorous studying, the graduate settled in for a weekend of *plebeian* socializing and television watching.

Synonyms: conventional; unrefined

a firmly held opinion, especially a religious belief

> Linus's central *dogma* was that children who believed in the Great Pumpkin would be rewarded.

Synonyms: creed; doctrines; teaching; tenet

**PLEBEIAN**

adj (plee bee uhn)

## DOGMATIC

adj (dahg maat ihk) (dawg maat ihk)

able to be molded, altered, or bent

The new material was very *plastic* and could be formed into products of vastly different shape.

Synonyms: adaptable; ductile; malleable; pliant

dictatorial in one's opinions

The dictator was *dogmatic*, claiming he, and only he, was right.

Synonyms: authoritarian; bossy; dictatorial; doctrinaire; domineering; imperious

**PLASTIC**

adj (plaa stihk)

to soothe or pacify

The burglar tried to *placate* the snarling dog by referring to it as a 'Nice Doggy' and offering it a treat.

Synonyms: appease; conciliate; mollify

## DROLL

adj (drohl)

amusing in a wry, subtle way

Although the play couldn't be described as hilarious, it was certainly *droll*.

Synonyms: comic; entertaining; funny; risible; witty

**PLACATE**

verb (play cayt)

profound, substantial; concise, succinct, to the point

Martha's *pithy* comments during the interview must have been impressive because she got the job.

Synonyms: brief; compact; laconic; terse

# DUPE

verb (doop)

to deceive

Bugs Bunny was able to *dupe* Elmer Fudd by dressing up as a lady rabbit.

Synonyms: beguile; betray; bluff; cozen; deceive; delude; fool; hoodwink; humbug; mislead; take in trick

**PITHY**

adj (pih thee)

calm and unemotional in temperament

Although the bomb could go off at any moment, the *phlegmatic* demolition expert remained calm and unafraid.

Synonyms: apathetic; calm; emotionless; impassive; indifferent; passionless; unemotional

## DYSPEPTIC

adj (dihs <u>pehp</u> tihk)

suffering from indigestion; gloomy and irritable

The *dyspeptic* young man cast a gloom over the party the minute he walked in.

Synonyms: acerb; melancholy; morose; solemn; sour

**PHLEGMATIC**

adj (flehg maa tihk)

## EBULLIENT

adj (ih <u>byool</u> yuhnt) (ih <u>buhl</u> yuhnt)

a person who is guided by materialism and is disdainful of intellectual or artistic values

The *philistine* never even glanced at the rare violin in his collection but instead kept an eye on its value and sold it at a profit.

Synonyms: boor; bourgeois; capitalist; clown; lout; materialist; vulgarian

exhilarated, full of enthusiasm and high spirits

The *ebullient* child exhausted the baby-sitter, who lacked the energy to keep up with her.

Synonyms: ardent; avid; bubbly; zestful

**PHILISTINE**

noun (fihl uh steen)

# ECLECTIC

adj (ih <u>klehk</u> tihk) (eh <u>klehk</u> tihk)

charity; a desire or effort to promote goodness

The Metropolitan Museum of Art owes much of its collection to the *philanthropy* of private collectors who willed their estates to the museum.

Synonyms: altruism; humanitarianism

selecting from or made up from a variety of sources

Budapest's architecture is an *eclectic* mix of eastern and western styles.

Synonyms: broad; catholic; selective

**PHILANTHROPY**

noun (fihl aan throh pee)

## EDIFY

verb (<u>eh</u> duh fie)

a compact or close-knit body of people, animals, or things

*A phalanx* of guards stood outside the prime minister's home day and night.

Synonyms: legion; mass

to instruct morally and spiritually

The guru was paid to *edify* the actress in the ways of Buddhism.

Synonyms: educate; enlighten; guide; teach

**PHALANX**

noun (fay laanks)

## EFFICACY

noun (<u>eh</u> fih kuh see)

to be present throughout, to permeate

Four spices—cumin, turmeric, coriander and cayenne—*pervade* almost every Indian dish, and give the cuisine its distinctive flavor.

Synonyms: imbue; infuse; penetrate; permeate; suffuse

effectiveness

> The *efficacy* of penicillin was unsurpassed when it was first introduced, completely eliminating almost all bacterial infections.

Synonyms: dynamism; effectiveness; efficiency; force; power; productiveness; proficiency; strength; vigor

**PERVADE**

verb (puhr vayd)

## EFFIGY

noun (eh fuh jee)

shrewd, astute, keen-witted

Inspector Poirot used his *perspicacious* mind to solve mysteries.

Synonyms: insightful; intelligent; sagacious

stuffed doll; likeness of a person

In England, *effigies* of the historic rebel Guy Fawkes are burned to celebrate his capture.

Synonyms: dummy; figure; image

**PERSPICACIOUS**

adj (puhr spuh kay shuhs)

## EFFRONTERY

noun (ih fruhnt uhr ee) (eh fruhnt uhr ee)

to penetrate

This miraculous new cleaning fluid is able to *permeate* stains and dissolve them in minutes!

Synonyms: imbue; infuse; pervade; suffuse

impudent boldness; audacity

The receptionist had the *effrontery* to laugh out loud when the CEO tripped over a computer wire and fell flat on his face.

Synonyms: brashness; gall; nerve; presumption; temerity

**PERMEATE**

verb (puhr mee ayt)

## **ELEGY**

noun (eh luh jee)

wandering from place to place, especially on foot

Elena's *peripatetic* meanderings took her all over the countryside in the summer months.

Synonyms: itinerant; nomadic; wayfaring

a sorrowful poem or speech

> Though Thomas Gray's *Elegy* is about death and loss, it urges its readers to endure this life, and to trust in spirituality.

Synonyms: dirge; lament

**PERIPATETIC**

adj (peh ruh puh teh tihk)

**ELOQUENT**

adj (ehl uh kwunt)

done in a routine way; indifferent

The machine-like teller processed the transaction and gave the waiting customer a *perfunctory* smile.

Synonyms: apathetic; automatic; mechanical

persuasive and moving, especially in speech

> The Gettysburg Address is moving not only because of its lofty sentiments but because of its *eloquent* words.

Synonyms: articulate; expressive; fluent; meaningful; significant; smooth-spoken

**PERFUNCTORY**

adj (pur funk tuhr ee)

## EMBELLISH

verb (ehm behl ihsh)

willing to betray one's trust

The actress's *perfidious* companion revealed all of her intimate secrets to the gossip columnist.

Synonyms: disloyal; faithless; traitorous; treacherous

to add ornamental or fictitious details

Britt *embellished* her résumé, hoping to make the lowly positions she had held seem more important.

Synonyms: adorn; bedeck; elaborate; embroider; enhance; exaggerate

**PERFIDIOUS**

adj (puhr fih dee uhs)

## EMULATE

verb (ehm yuh layt)

to wander from place to place; to travel, especially on foot

Shivani enjoyed *peregrinating* the expansive grounds of Central Park.

Synonyms: journey; traverse; trek

to copy, to try to equal or excel

The graduate student sought to *emulate* his professor in every way, copying not only how she taught but also how she conducted herself outside of class.

Synonyms: ape; imitate; simulate

**PEREGRINATE**

verb (peh ruh gruh nayt)

## ENCOMIUM

noun (ehn koh me uhm)

an oppressive lack of resources (as money); severe poverty

Once a famous actor, he eventually died in *penury* and anonymity.

Synonyms: destitution; impoverishment

warm praise

Georgias's "*Encomium* to Helen" was written as a tribute to Helen of Troy.

Synonyms: citation; eulogy; panegyric; salutation; tribute

**PENURY**

noun (pehn yuh ree)

## ENDEMIC

adj (ehn <u>deh</u> mihk)

having bad connotations; disparaging

The teacher scolded Mark for his unduly *pejorative* comments about his classmate's presentation.

Synonyms: belittling; dismissive; insulting

belonging to a particular area; inherent

The health department determined that the outbreak was *endemic* to the small village, so it quarantined the inhabitants before the virus could spread.

Synonyms: indigenous; local; native

**PEJORATIVE**

adj (peh jaw ruh tihv)

## ENERVATE

verb (ehn uhr vayt)

someone who shows off learning

The graduate instructor's tedious and excessive commentary on the subject soon gained her a reputation as a *pedant*.

Synonyms: doctrinaire; nit-picker; pedagogue; scholar; schoolmaster; sophist

to reduce in strength

> The guerrillas hoped that a series of surprise attacks would *enervate* the regular army.

Synonyms: debilitate; enfeeble; sap; weaken

**PEDANT**

noun (peh daant)

## ENGENDER

verb (ehn jehn duhr)

minor sin or offense

Gabriel tends to harp on his brother's *peccadillos* and never lets him live them down.

Synonyms: failing; fault; lapse; misstep

to produce, cause, or bring about

His fear and hatred of clowns was *engendered* when he witnessed a bank robbery carried out by five men wearing clown suits and make-up.

Synonyms: beget; generate; procreate; proliferate; reproduce; spawn

**PECCADILLO**

noun (pehk uh dihl loh)

## ENIGMA

noun (ih nig muh)

causing disease

Bina's research on the origins of *pathogenic* microorganisms should help stop the spread of disease.

Synonyms: infecting; noxious

a puzzle, a mystery

Speaking in riddles and dressed in old robes, the artist gained a reputation as something of an *enigma*.

Synonyms: conundrum; perplexity

**PATHOGENIC**

adj (paa thoh jehn ihk)

## ENUMERATE

verb (ih noo muhr ayt)

piece of literature or music imitating other works

The singer's clever *pastiche* of the well-known children's story had the audience rolling in the aisles.

Synonyms: medley; spoof

to count, list, itemize

Before making his decision, Jacob asked the waiter to *enumerate* the different varieties of ice cream that the restaurant carried.

Synonyms: catalog; index; tabulate

**PASTICHE**

noun (pah steesh)

## EPHEMERAL

adj (ih fehm uhr uhl)

to ward off or deflect, especially by a quick-witted answer

Kari *parried* every question the army officers fired at her, much to their frustration.

Synonyms: avoid; evade; repel

lasting a short time

> The lives of mayflies seem *ephemeral* to us, since the flies' average life span is a matter of hours.

Synonyms: evanescent; fleeting; momentary; transient

**PARRY**

verb (paar ree)

## EPICURE

noun (eh pih kyoor) (eh pih kyuhr)

discussion, usually between enemies

The *parley* between the rival cheerleading teams resulted in neither side admitting that they copied the other's dance moves.

Synonyms: debate; dialogue; negotiations; talks

person with refined taste in food and wine

Niren is an *epicure* who always throws the most splendid dinner parties.

Synonyms: bon vivant; connoisseur; gastronome; gastronomer; gastronomist; gourmand; gourmet

**PARLEY**

noun (par lee)

**EQUIVOCATE**

verb (ih <u>kwihv</u> uh kayt)

an outcast

Once he betrayed those in his community, he was banished and lived the life of a *pariah.*

Synonyms: castaway; derelict; leper; offscouring; untouchable

to use expressions of double meaning in order to mislead

> When faced with criticism of his policies, the politician *equivocated* and left all parties thinking he agreed with them.

Synonyms: hedge; waffle

**PARIAH**

noun (puh rie uh)

**ERRATIC**

adj (ih raat ihk)

to trim off excess, reduce

The cook's hands were sore after she *pared* hundreds of potatoes for the banquet.

Synonyms: clip; peel

wandering and unpredictable

The plot seemed predictable until it suddenly took a series of *erratic* turns that surprised the audience.

Synonyms: capricious; inconstant; irresolute; whimsical

**PARE**

verb (payr)

**ERSATZ**

adj (<u>uhr</u> sats) (uhr <u>sats</u>)

model of excellence or perfection

He is the *paragon* of what a judge should be: honest, intelligent, hardworking, and just.

Synonyms: apotheosis; ideal; quintessence; standard

fake, artificial

Edda, a fashion maven, knew instantly that her friend's new Kate Spade bag was really an *ersatz* version purchased on the street.

Synonyms: false; imitation

**PARAGON**

noun (par uh gohn)

## ERUDITE

adj (<u>ehr</u> yuh dite) (<u>ehr</u> uh dite)

a contradiction or dilemma

It is a *paradox* that those most in need of medical attention are often those least able to obtain it.

Synonyms: ambiguity; incongruity

learned, scholarly, bookish

The annual meeting of philosophy professors was a gathering of the most *erudite*, well-published individuals in the field.

Synonyms: learned; scholastic; wise

**PARADOX**

noun (par uh doks)

**ESCHEW**

verb (ehs <u>choo</u>)

impressive array

Her résumé indicates a *panoply* of skills and accomplishments.

Synonyms: array; display; range

to shun, to avoid (as something wrong or distasteful)

The filmmaker *eschewed* artificial light for her actors, resulting in a stark movie style.

Synonyms: avoid; elude; escape; evade

**PANOPLY**

noun (p̄aa nuh plee)

## ESOTERIC

adj (eh suh <u>tehr</u> ihk)

elaborate praise; formal hymn of praise

The director's *panegyric* for the donor who kept his charity going was heart-warming.

Synonyms: compliment; homage

known or understood only by a few

> Only a handful of experts are knowledgeable about the *esoteric* world of particle physics.

Synonyms: abstruse; arcane; obscure

**PANEGYRIC**

noun (paan uh jeer ihk)

## ESTIMABLE

adj (<u>eh</u> stuh muh buhl)

flamboyance or dash in style and action; verve

Leah has such *panache* when planning parties, even when they're last-minute affairs.

Synonym: flair

admirable

> Most people consider it *estimable* that Mother Teresa spent her life helping the poor of India.

Synonyms: admirable; commendable; creditable; honorable; laudable; meritorious; praiseworthy; respectable; venerable; worthy

**PANACHE**

noun (puh nahsh)

**ETHOS**

noun (<u>ee</u> thohs)

lacking color or liveliness

The old drugstore's *pallid* window could not compete with Wal-Mart's extravagant display next door.

Synonyms: ashen; blanched; ghostly; pale; wan

beliefs or character of a group

It is the Boy Scouts' *ethos* that one should always be prepared.

Synonyms: culture; ethic; philosophy

**PALLID**

adj (paa lihd)

## EULOGY

noun (yoo luh jee)

to make less serious; ease

The alleged crime was so vicious that the defense lawyer could not *palliate* it for the jury.

Synonyms: alleviate; assuage; extenuate; mitigate

speech in praise of someone

His best friend gave the *eulogy*, outlining his many achievements and talents.

Synonyms: encomium; elegy; panegyric

**PALLIATE**

verb (paa lee ayt)

## EUPHEMISM

noun (yoo fum ih zuhm)

relating to a palace; magnificent

After living in a cramped studio apartment for years, Siobhan thought the modest one-bedroom looked downright *palatial.*

Synonyms: grand; stately

use of an inoffensive word or phrase in place of a more distasteful one

> The funeral director preferred to use the *euphemism* 'sleeping' instead of the word 'dead.'

**PALATIAL**

adj (puh lay shuhl)

## EUPHONY

noun (<u>yoo</u> fuh nee)

agitated, overdone

The lawyer's *overwrought* voice on the phone made her clients worry about the outcome of their case.

Synonyms: elaborate; excited; nervous; ornate

pleasant, harmonious sound

To their loving parents, the children's orchestra performance sounded like *euphony*, although an outside observer would have probably called it a cacophony.

Synonyms: harmony; melody; music; sweetness

**OVERWROUGHT**

adj (oh vuhr rawt)

## EXACERBATE

verb (ihg <u>zaas</u> uhr bayt)

excessive showiness

The *ostentation* of The Sun King's court is evident in the lavish decoration and luxuriousness of his palace at Versailles.

Synonyms: conspicuousness; flashiness; pretentiousness; showiness

to make worse

> It is unwise to take aspirin to try to relieve heartburn since instead of providing relief it will only *exacerbate* the problem.

Synonyms: aggravate; annoy; intensify; irritate; provoke

**OSTENTATION**

noun (ah stehn tay shuhn)

## EXCULPATE

verb (ehk skuhl payt) (ihk skuhl payt)

apparent

The *ostensible* reason for his visit was to borrow a book, but he secretly wanted to chat with the lovely Wanda.

Synonyms: represented; supposed; surface

to clear from blame, to prove innocent

> The legal system is intended to convict those who are guilty and *exculpate* those who are innocent.

Synonyms: absolve; acquit; clear; exonerate; vindicate

**OSTENSIBLE**

adj (ah stehn sih buhl)

## EXIGENT

adj (ehk suh juhnt)

to change into bone; to become hardened or set in a rigid conventional pattern

The forensics expert ascertained the body's age based on the degree to which the facial structure had *ossified*.

urgent; requiring immediate action

The patient was losing blood so rapidly that it was *exigent* to stop the source of the bleeding.

Synonyms: critical; imperative; needed; urgent

**OSSIFY**

verb (ah sih fie)

## EXONERATE

verb (ihg <u>zahn</u> uh rayt)

pompous

Roberto soon grew tired of his date's *orotund* babble about her new job, and decided their first date would probably be their last.

Synonyms: aureate; bombastic; declamatory; euphuistic; flowery; grandiloquent; magniloquent; oratorical; overblown; sonorous

to clear of blame

The fugitive was *exonerated* when another criminal confessed to committing the crime.

Synonyms: absolve; acquit; clear; exculpate; vindicate

**OROTUND**

adj (o̅r̅ uh tuhnd) (a̅h̅ ruh tuhnd)

## EXPLICIT

adj (ehk <u>splih</u> siht)

public disgrace

After the scheme to embezzle the elderly was made public, the treasurer resigned in utter *opprobrium.*

Synonyms: discredit; disgrace; dishonor; disrepute; ignominy; infamy; obloquy; shame

clearly stated or shown; forthright in expression

In Reading Comprehension, questions that ask directly about a detail in the passage are sometimes called *Explicit* Text questions.

Synonyms: candid; clear-cut; definite; definitive; express; frank; specific; straightforward; unambiguous; unequivocal

**OPPROBRIUM**

noun (uh pro bree uhm)

# EXPONENT

noun (ihk <u>spoh</u> nuhnt) (<u>ehk</u> spoh nuhnt)

to express an opinion

At the "Let's Chat Talk Show," the audience member *opined* that the guest was in the wrong.

Synonyms: point out; voice

one who champions or advocates

The vice president was an enthusiastic *exponent* of computer technology.

Synonyms: representative; supporter

**OPINE**

verb (oh pīen)

**EXPURGATE**

verb (<u>ehk</u> spuhr gayt)

impossible to see through, preventing the passage of light

The heavy build-up of dirt and grime on the windows made them almost *opaque*.

Synonym: obscure

to censor

Government propagandists *expurgated* all negative references to the dictator from the film.

Synonyms: cut; sanitize

**OPAQUE**

adj (oh payk)

## FALLOW

adj (<u>faa</u> loh)

troublesome and oppressive; burdensome

The assignment was so extensive and difficult to manage that it proved *onerous* to the team in charge of it.

Synonyms: arduous; backbreaking; burdensome; cumbersome; difficult; exacting; formidable; hard; laborious; oppressive; rigorous; taxing; trying

dormant, unused

This field should lie *fallow* for a year so the soil does not become completely depleted.

Synonyms: idle; inactive; unseeded

**ONEROUS**

adj (ōh neh ruhs)

## FANATICAL

adj (fuh <u>nah</u> tih kuhl)

too helpful, meddlesome

While planning her wedding, Maya discovered just how *officious* her future mother-in-law could be.

Synonyms: eager; intrusive; unwanted

acting excessively enthusiastic; filled with extreme, unquestioned devotion

The stormtroopers were *fanatical* in their devotion to the Emperor, readily sacrificing their lives for him.

Synonyms: extremist; fiery; frenzied; zealous

**OFFICIOUS**

adj (uh fihsh uhs)

## FATUOUS

adj (fah choo uhs)

to stop up, prevent the passage of

A shadow is thrown across the Earth's surface during a solar eclipse, when the light from the sun is *occluded* by the moon.

Synonyms: barricade; block; close; obstruct

stupid; foolishly self-satisfied

Ted's *fatuous* comments always embarrassed his keen-witted wife at parties.

Synonyms: absurd; ludicrous; preposterous; ridiculous; silly

**OCCLUDE**

verb (uh klood)

## FAWN

verb (fahn)

to prevent; to make unnecessary

The river was shallow enough to wade across at many points, which *obviated* the need for a bridge.

Synonyms: forestall; preclude; prohibit

to grovel

The understudy *fawned* over the director in hopes of being cast in the part on a permanent basis.

Synonyms: bootlick; grovel; pander; toady

**OBVIATE**

verb (ahb vee ayt)

**FECUND**

adj (fee kuhnd) (feh kuhnd)

stubborn, unyielding

The *obstinate* child could not be made to eat any food that he perceived to be 'yucky.'

Synonyms: intransigent; mulish; persistent; pertinacious; stubborn; tenacious

fertile, fruitful, productive

The *fecund* couple yielded a total of 20 children.

Synonyms: flourishing; prolific

**OBSTINATE**

adj (ahb stih nuht)

## FERVID

adj (fuhr vihd)

overly submissive and eager to please

The *obsequious* new associate made sure to compliment her supervisor's tie and agree with him on every issue.

Synonyms: compliant; deferential; servile; subservient

intensely emotional, feverish

The fans of Maria Callas were particularly *fervid*, doing anything to catch a glimpse of the great opera singer.

Synonyms: burning; impassioned; passionate; vehement; zealous

**OBSEQUIOUS**

adj (uhb see kwee uhs)

## FETID

adj (<u>feh</u> tihd)

indirect, evasive; misleading, devious

Usually open and friendly, Reinaldo has been behaving in a curiously *oblique* manner lately.

Synonyms: glancing; slanted; tangential

foul-smelling, putrid

The *fetid* stench from the outhouse caused Francesca to wrinkle her nose in disgust.

Synonyms: funky; malodorous; noisome; rank; stinky

**OBLIQUE**

adj (oh bleek)

**FLAG**

verb (flaag)

hardened in feeling, resistant to persuasion

The president was completely *obdurate* on the issue, and no amount of persuasion would change his mind.

Synonyms: inflexible; intransigent; recalcitrant; tenacious; unyielding

to decline in vigor, strength, or interest

The marathon runner slowed down as his strength *flagged*.

Synonyms: dwindle; ebb; slacken; subside; wane

**OBDURATE**

adj (ahb duhr uht)

**FLORID**

adj (<u>flohr</u> ihd) (<u>flahr</u> ihd)

coin collecting

Tomas's passion for *numismatics* has resulted in an impressive collection of coins from all over the world.

excessively decorated or embellished

> The palace had been decorated in an excessively *florid* style; every surface had been carved and gilded.

Synonyms: Baroque; elaborate; flamboyant; ornate; ostentatious; Rococo

**NUMISMATICS**

noun (nu miz maa tiks)

## FOMENT

verb (foh <u>mehnt</u>)

a subtle expression of meaning or quality

The scholars argued for hours over tiny *nuances* in the interpretation of the last line of the poem.

Synonyms: gradation; subtlety; tone

to arouse or incite

The rebels tried to *foment* revolution through their attacks on the government.

Synonyms: agitate; impassion; inflame; instigate; kindle

**NUANCE**

noun (n$\overline{oo}$ ahns)

**FORD**

verb (fohrd)

existing in name only; negligible

A *nominal* member of the high school yearbook committee, she rarely attends meetings.

Synonyms: minimal; titular

to cross a body of water by wading

> Because of the recent torrential rains, the cowboys were unable to *ford* the swollen river.

Synonyms: traverse; wade

**NOMINAL**

adj (nah mihn uhl)

## FORESTALL

verb (fohr stahl)

stinking, putrid

A dead mouse trapped in your walls produces a *noisome* odor.

Synonyms: disgusting; foul; malodorous

to prevent, delay; anticipate

The landlord *forestalled* T.J.'s attempt to avoid paying the rent by waiting for him outside his door.

Synonyms: avert; deter; hinder; obviate; preclude

**NOISOME**

adj (noy suhm)

## FORTUITOUS

adj (fohr <u>too</u> ih tuhs)

to irritate

I don't particularly like having blue hair—I just do it to *nettle* my parents.

Synonyms: annoy; vex

happening by chance, fortunate

It was *fortuitous* that he won the lotto just before he had to pay back his loans.

Synonyms: chance; fortunate; haphazard; lucky; propitious; prosperous

**NETTLE**

verb (neh tuhl)

## FRACTIOUS

adj (fraak shuhs)

novice, beginner

A relative *neophyte* at bowling, Rodolfo rolled all of his balls into the gutter.

Synonyms: apprentice; greenhorn; tyro

unruly, rebellious

The general had a hard time maintaining discipline among his *fractious* troops.

Synonyms: contentious; cranky; peevish; quarrelsome

**NEOPHYTE**

noun (nee oh fiet)

# FRENETIC

adj (fruh neht ihk)

new word or expression

Aunt Mable simply does not understand today's youth; she is perplexed by their clothing, music, and *neologisms.*

Synonyms: slang; slip-of-the-tongue

frantic, frenzied

The employee's *frenetic* schedule left her little time to socialize.

Synonym: corybantic; delirious; feverish; mad; rabid; wild

**NEOLOGISM**

noun (nee ah luh ji zuhm)

## FRUGALITY

noun (fru gaa luh tee)

starting to develop, coming into existence

The advertising campaign was still in a *nascent* stage, and nothing had been finalized yet.

Synonyms: embryonic; emerging; inchoate; incipient

tendency to be thrifty or cheap

Scrooge McDuck's *frugality* was so great that he accumulated enough wealth to fill a giant storehouse with money.

Synonyms: cheapness; economy; parsimony

**NASCENT**

adj (nay sehnt)

**FURTIVE**

adj (<u>fuhr</u> tihv)

lacking sophistication or experience

Inexperienced writers often are *naïve* and assume that big words make them sound smarter.

Synonyms: artless; credulous; guileless; ingenuous; simple; unaffected; unsophisticated

secret, stealthy

Glenn was *furtive* when he peered out of the corner of his eye at the stunningly beautiful model.

Synonyms: clandestine; covert; shifty; surreptitious; underhand

**NAÏVE**

adj (nah $\overline{ee}$v)

**GAMBOL**

verb (gaam buhl)

lowest point

As Joey waited in line to audition for the diaper commercial, he realized he had reached the *nadir* of his acting career.

Synonyms: bottom; depth; pit

to dance or skip around playfully

From her office, Amy enviously watched the playful puppies *gambol* around Central Park.

Synonyms: caper; cavort; frisk; frolic; rollick; romp

**NADIR**

noun (nay dihr) (nay duhr)

## GARNER

verb (<u>gahr</u> nuhr)

lacking foresight, having a narrow view or long-range perspective

Not wanting to spend a lot of money up front, the *myopic* business owner would likely suffer the consequences later.

Synonyms: short-sighted; unthinking

to gather and store

> The director managed to *garner* financial backing from several different sources for his next project.

Synonyms: amass; acquire; glean; harvest; reap

**MYOPIC**

adj (mie ahp ihk) (mie oh pihk)

## GARRULOUS

adj (<u>gaar</u> uh luhs) (<u>gaar</u> yuh luhs)

diverse

Ken opened the hotel room window, letting in the *multifarious* noises of the great city.

Synonyms: assorted; indiscriminate; heterogeneous; legion; motley; multifold; multiform; multiplex; multivarious; populous; varied

tending to talk a lot

The *garrulous* parakeet distracted its owner with its continuous talking.

Synonyms: effusive; loquacious

**MULTIFARIOUS**

adj (muhl tuh faar ee uhs)

## GESTATION

noun (jeh <u>stay</u> shuhn)

fixed customs or manners; moral attitudes

In keeping with the *mores* of ancient Roman society, Nero held a celebration every weekend.

Synonyms: conventions; practices

growth process from conception to birth

The longer the *gestation* period of an organism, the more developed the baby is at birth.

Synonyms: development; gravidity; pregnancy

**MORES**

noun (mawr ayz)

## GLIB

adj (glihb)

no variation, tediously the same

The *monotony* of the sound of the dripping faucet almost drove the research assistant crazy.

Synonyms: drone; tedium

fluent in an insincere manner; offhand, casual

> The slimy politician managed to continue gaining supporters because he was a *glib* speaker.

Synonyms: easy; superficial

**MONOTONY**

noun (muh naht nee)

## GLOWER

verb (<u>glow</u> uhr)

extremely plain or secluded, as in a monastery

The philosopher retired to his *monastic* lodgings to contemplate life free from any worldly distraction.

Synonyms: austere; contemplative; disciplined; regimented; self-abnegating

to glare; stare angrily and intensely

The cranky waiter *glowered* at the indecisive customer.

Synonyms: frown; lower; scowl

**MONASTIC**

adj (muh naas tihk)

## GRADATION

noun (gray <u>day</u> shuhn)

to shed hair, skin, or an outer layer periodically

The snake *molted* its skin and left it behind in a crumpled mass.

Synonyms: cast; defoliate; desquamate

process occurring by regular degrees or stages; variation in color

The paint store offers so many different *gradations* of red that it's impossible to choose among them.

Synonyms: nuance; shade; step; subtlety

**MOLT**

verb (muhlt)

**GREGARIOUS**

adj (greh gayr ee uhs)

to calm or make less severe

Their argument was so intense that is was difficult to believe any compromise would *mollify* them.

Synonyms: appease; assuage; conciliate; pacify

outgoing, sociable

She was so *gregarious* that when she found herself alone she felt quite sad.

Synonyms: affable; communicative; congenial; sociable

**MOLLIFY**

verb (mahl uh fie)

## GRIEVOUS

adj (gree vuhs)

to soften, to lessen

A judge may *mitigate* a sentence if she decides that a person committed a crime out of need.

Synonyms: allay; alleviate; assuage; ease; lighten; moderate; mollify; palliate; temper

causing grief or sorrow; serious and distressing

Maude and Bertha sobbed loudly throughout the *grievous* event.

Synonyms: dire; dolorous; grave; mournful

**MITIGATE**

verb (miht ih gayt)

**GROVEL**

verb (<u>grah</u> vuhl)

a written note or letter

Priscilla spent hours composing a romantic *missive* for Elvis.

Synonym: message

to humble oneself in a demeaning way

Thor *groveled* to his ex-girlfriend, hoping she would take him back.

Synonyms: bootlick; cringe; fawn; kowtow; toady

**MISSIVE**

noun (mihs ihv)

## GUILE

noun (<u>gie</u> uhl)

a person who dislikes others

The Grinch was such a *misanthrope* that even the sight of children singing made him angry.

Synonym: curmudgeon

deceit, trickery

Since he was not fast enough to catch the roadrunner on foot, the coyote resorted to *guile* in an effort to trap his enemy.

Synonyms: artifice; chicanery; connivery; duplicity

**MISANTHROPE**

noun (mihs ahn throhp)

## GULLIBLE

adj (guh luh buhl)

frivolity, gaiety, laughter

Vera's hilarious jokes contributed to the general *mirth* at the dinner party.

Synonyms: glee; hilarity; jollity; merriment

easily deceived

The con man pretended to be a bank officer so as to fool *gullible* bank customers into giving him their account information.

Synonyms: credulous; exploitable; naïve

**MIRTH**

noun (muhrth)

**HAPLESS**

adj (haap luhs)

to operate against, work against

Lenin *militated* against the tsar for years before he overthrew him and established the Soviet Union.

Synonyms: influence; affect; change

unfortunate, having bad luck

I wish someone would give that poor, *hapless* soul some food and shelter.

Synonyms: ill-fated; ill-starred; jinxed; luckless; unlucky

**MILITATE**

verb (mihl ih tayt)

## HEGEMONY

noun (hih jeh muh nee)

extremely careful, fastidious, painstaking

To find all the clues at the crime scene, the *meticulous* investigators examined every inch of the area.

Synonyms: finicky; fussy; picky; precise; punctilious; scrupulous

the domination of one state or group over its allies

When Germany claimed *hegemony* over Russia, Stalin was outraged.

Synonyms: authority; power

**METICULOUS**

adj (mih tihk yuh luhs)

## HERMETIC

adj (huhr <u>meh</u> tihk)

---

figure of speech comparing two different things

The *metaphor* "a sea of troubles" suggests a lot of troubles by comparing their number to the vastness of the sea.

Synonyms: allegory; analogy; simile; symbol

tightly sealed

The *hermetic* seal of the jar proved impossible to break.

Synonyms: airtight; impervious; watertight

**METAPHOR**

noun (meht uh fohr) (meht uh fuhr)

## HETEROGENEOUS

adj (heh tuh ruh jee nee uhs) (he truh jee nyuhs)

gaudy; falsely attractive

The casino's *meretricious* decor horrified the cultivated interior designer.

Synonyms: flashy; insincere; loud; specious; tawdry

composed of unlike parts, different, diverse

The United Nations is by nature a *heterogeneous* body.

Synonyms: assorted; miscellaneous; mixed; motley; varied

**MERETRICIOUS**

adj (mehr ih trihsh uhs)

# HOARY

adj (hohr ee) (haw ree)

quick, shrewd, and unpredictable

Her *mercurial* personality made it difficult to guess how she would react to the bad news.

Synonyms: clever; crafty; volatile; whimsical

very old; whitish or gray from age

The old man's *hoary* beard contrasted starkly with the new stubble of his teenage grandson.

Synonyms: ancient; antediluvian; antique; venerable; vintage

**MERCURIAL**

adj (muhr kyoor ee uhl)

## HOMOGENOUS

adj (huh mah juhn uhs)

beggar

"Please, sir, can you spare a dime?" begged the *mendicant* as the businessman walked past.

Synonyms: panhandler; pauper

of a similar kind

The class was fairly *homogenous* since almost all of the students were journalism majors.

Synonyms: consistent; standardized; uniform; unvarying

**MENDICANT**

noun (mehn dih kuhnt)

## HUSBAND

verb (huhz buhnd)

dishonest

So many of her stories were *mendacious* that I decided she must be a pathological liar.

Synonyms: deceitful; false; lying; untruthful

to manage economically; to use sparingly

The cyclist paced herself at the start of the race, knowing that if she *husbanded* her resources she'd have the strength to break out of the pack later on.

Synonym: conserve

**MENDACIOUS**

adj (mehn day shuhs)

**HYPERBOLE**

noun (hie <u>puhr</u> boh lee)

overly sentimental

The mother's death should have been a touching scene, but the movie's treatment of it was so *maudlin* that, instead of making the audience cry, it made them cringe.

Synonyms: bathetic; mawkish; saccharine; weepy

purposeful exaggeration for effect

When the mayor claimed his town was one of the seven wonders of the world, outsiders classified his statement as a *hyperbole*.

Synonyms: embellishment; inflation; magnification

**MAUDLIN**

adj (mawd lihn)

## ICONOCLAST

noun (ie kahn uh klaast)

strict disciplinarian; one who rigidly follows rules

A complete *martinet*, the official insisted that Pete fill out all the forms again even though he was already familiar with his case.

Synonyms: dictator; stickler; tyrant

one who opposes established beliefs, customs, and institutions

His lack of regard for traditional beliefs soon established him as an *iconoclast*.

Synonyms: maverick; nonconformist; rebel; revolutionary

**MARTINET**

noun (mahr tihn eht)

## IDIOSYNCRACY

noun (ih dee uh sihn kruh see)

to damage, deface; spoil

Telephone poles *mar* the natural beauty of the countryside.

Synonyms: blemish; disfigure; impair; injure; scar

peculiarity of temperament, eccentricity

His numerous *idiosyncrasies* included a fondness for wearing bright green shoes with mauve socks.

Synonyms: humor; oddity; quirk

**MAR**

verb (mahr)

## IGNOBLE

adj (ihg noh buhl)

artificial or stilted in character

The portrait is an example of the *mannered* style that was favored in that era.

Synonyms: affected; unnatural

having low moral standards, not noble in character; mean

> The photographer was paid a princely sum for the picture of the self-proclaimed ethicist in the *ignoble* act of pick-pocketing.

Synonyms: lowly; vulgar

**MANNERED**

adj (maan uhrd)

## IMBUE

verb (ihm <u>byoo</u>)

capable of being shaped

Gold is the most *malleable* of precious metals; it can easily be formed into almost any shape.

Synonyms: adaptable; ductile; plastic; pliable; pliant

to infuse; dye, wet, moisten

Marcia struggled to *imbue* her children with decent values, a difficult task in this day and age.

Synonyms: charge; freight; impregnate; permeate; pervade

**MALLEABLE**

adj (mah lee uh buhl) (mal yuh buhl) (mah luh buhl)

## IMPASSE

noun (ihm paas) (ihm pass)

to evade responsibility by pretending to be ill

A common way to avoid the draft was by *malingering*—pretending to be mentally or physically ill so as to avoid being taken by the Army.

Synonyms: shirk; slack

blocked path; dilemma with no solution

The rock slide produced an *impasse*, so no one could proceed further on the road.

Synonyms: cul-de-sac; deadlock; stalemate

**MALINGER**

verb (muh ling guhr)

# IMPECUNIOUS

adj (ihm pih kyoo nyuhs) (ihm pih kyoo nee uhs)

a curse; a wish of evil upon another

The frog prince looked for a princess to kiss him and put an end to the witch's *malediction.*

Synonyms: anathema; imprecation

poor, having no money

> After the stock market crashed, many former millionaires found themselves *impecunious*.

Synonyms: destitute; impoverished; indigent; needy; penniless

**MALEDICTION**

noun (maal ih dihk shun)

## IMPERTURBABLE

adj (im puhr tuhr buh buhl)

powerful or influential person

The entertainment *magnate* bought two cable TV stations to add to his collection of magazines and publishing houses.

Synonyms: dignitary; luminary; nabob; potentate; tycoon

not capable of being disturbed

> The counselor had so much experience dealing with distraught children that she was *imperturbable*, even when faced with the wildest tantrums.

Synonyms: composed; dispassionate; impassive; serene; stoical

**MAGNATE**

noun (maag nayt) (maag niht)

## IMPERVIOUS

adj (ihm puhr vee uhs)

whirlpool; turmoil; agitated state of mind

The transportation system of the city had collapsed in the *maelstrom* of war.

Synonyms: Charybdis; eddy; turbulence

impossible to penetrate; incapable of being affected

A good raincoat will be *impervious* to moisture.

Synonyms: impregnable; resistant

**MAELSTROM**

noun (mayl struhm)

## IMPETUOUS

adj (ihm <u>peh</u> choo uhs) (ihm <u>pehch</u> wuhs)

plot or scheme

Tired of his enemies' endless *machinations* to remove him from the throne, the king had them executed.

Synonyms: cabal; conspiracy; design; intrigue

quick to act without thinking

It is not good for an investment broker to be *impetuous* since much thought should be given to all the possible options.

Synonyms: impulsive; precipitate; rash; reckless; spontaneous

**MACHINATION**

noun (mahk uh nay shuhn)

bright, brilliant, glowing

The park was bathed in *luminous* sunshine that warmed the bodies and the souls of the visitors.

Synonyms: incandescent; lucent; lustrous; radiant; resplendent

## IMPIOUS

adj (ihm pee uhs)(ihm pie uhs)

not devout in religion

The nun cut herself off from her *impious* family after she entered the convent.

Synonyms: immoral; irreverent; profane

**LUMINOUS**

adj (lo͞o muhn uhs)

## IMPLACABLE

adj (ihm <u>play</u> kuh buhl) (ihm <u>plaa</u> kuh buhl)

to move slowly and awkwardly

The bear *lumbered* towards the garbage, drooling at the prospect of the Big Mac leftovers he smelled.

Synonyms: galumph; hulk; lurch; stumble

unable to be calmed down or made peaceful

His rage at the betrayal was so great that he remained *implacable* for weeks.

Synonyms: inexorable; intransigent; irreconcilable; relentless; remorseless; unforgiving; unrelenting

**LUMBER**

verb (luhm buhr)

## IMPRECATION

noun (ihm prih kay shuhn)

sorrowful, mournful; dismal

Irish wakes are a rousing departure from the *lugubrious* funeral services to which most people are accustomed.

Synonyms: funereal; gloomy; melancholy; somber; woeful

a curse

Spouting violent *imprecations*, Hank searched for the person who had vandalized his truck.

Synonym: damnation

**LUGUBRIOUS**

adj (loo goo bree uhs)

## IMPUGN

verb (ihm <u>pyoon</u>)

clear and easily understood

The explanations were written in a simple and *lucid* manner so that students were immediately able to apply what they had learned.

Synonyms: clear; coherent; explicit; intelligible; limpid

to call into question; to attack verbally

"How dare you *impugn* my motives?" protested the lawyer, on being accused of ambulance chasing.

Synonyms: challenge; dispute

**LUCID**

adj (l$\overline{oo}$ sihd)

## INCARNADINE

adj (in <u>car</u> nuh deen)

talkative

She is naturally *loquacious*, which is a problem in situations where listening is more important than talking.

Synonyms: effusive; garrulous; verbose

blood-red in color

At his mother's mention of his baby pictures, the shy boy's cheeks turned *incarnadine* with embarrassment.

Synonyms: reddened; ruby; ruddy

**LOQUACIOUS**

adj (loh kway shuhs)

## INCHOATE

adj (ihn <u>koh</u> uht)

discolored from a bruise; pale; reddened with anger

André was *livid* when he discovered that someone had spilled grape juice all over his cashmere coat.

Synonyms: ashen; black-and-blue; furious; pallid

not fully formed, disorganized

The ideas expressed in Nietzsche's mature work also appear in an *inchoate* form in his earliest writing.

Synonyms: amorphous; incoherent; incomplete; unorganized

**LIVID**

adj (lih vihd)

## INCULCATE

verb (ihn kuhl kayt) (ihn kuhl kayt)

lacking energy and enthusiasm

*Listless* and depressed after breaking up with his girlfriend, Raj spent his days moping on the couch.

Synonyms: fainéant; indolent; languid; lethargic; sluggish

to teach, impress in the mind

Most parents *inculcate* their children with their beliefs and ideas instead of allowing their children to develop their own values.

Synonyms: implant; indoctrinate; instill; preach

**LISTLESS**

adj (lihst lihs)

## INDOLENT

adj (<u>ihn</u> duh luhnt)

easily flexed, limber, agile

The *lissome* yoga instructor twisted herself into shapes that her students could only dream of.

Synonyms: graceful; lithe; supple

habitually lazy, idle

Her *indolent* ways got her fired from many jobs.

Synonyms: lethargic; slothful; sluggish

**LISSOME**

adj (lihs uhm)

## INEXORABLE

adj (ihn ehk suhr uh buhl)

to treat as a celebrity

After the success of his novel, the author was *lionized* by the press.

Synonyms: feast; honor; ply; regale

inflexible, unyielding

The *inexorable* force of the twister swept away their house.

Synonyms: adamant; obdurate; relentless

**LIONIZE**

verb (lie uhn iez)

## INGENUOUS

adj (ihn <u>jehn</u> yoo uhs)

clear, transparent

Fernando could see all the way to the bottom through the pond's *limpid* water.

Synonyms: lucid; pellucid; serene

showing innocence or childlike simplicity

> She was so *ingenuous* that her friends feared that her innocence and trustfulness would be exploited when she visited the big city.

Synonyms: artless; guileless; innocent; naïve; simple; unaffected

---

**LIMPID**

adj (lim pihd)

## INGRATE

noun (<u>ihn</u> grayt)

immoral; unrestrained by society

Religious citizens were outraged by the *licentious* exploits of the free-spirited artists living in town.

Synonyms: lewd; wanton

ungrateful person

When none of her relatives thanked her for the fruitcakes she had sent them, Audrey condemned them all as *ingrates*.

Synonyms: cad; churl

**LICENTIOUS**

adj (lie sehn shuhs)

## INGRATIATE

verb (ihn <u>gray</u> shee ayt)

a free thinker, usually used disparagingly; one without moral restraint

The *libertine* took pleasure in gambling away his family's money.

Synonym: hedonist

to gain favor with another by deliberate effort; to seek to please somebody so as to gain an advantage

> The new intern tried to *ingratiate* herself with the managers so that they might consider her for a future job.

Synonyms: curry favor; flatter

**LIBERTINE**

noun (lib uhr teen)

## INIMICAL

adj (ih <u>nihm</u> ih kuhl)

tolerant, broad-minded; generous, lavish

Cali's *liberal* parents trusted her and allowed her to manage her own affairs to a large extent.

Synonyms: bounteous; latitudinarian; munificent; permissive; progressive

hostile, unfriendly

Even though a cease-fire had been in place for months, the two sides were still *inimical* to each other.

Synonyms: adverse; antagonistic; dissident; recalcitrant

**LIBERAL**

adj (lihb uh ruhl) (lihb ruhl)

**INIQUITY**

noun (ih nihk wih tee)

an inappropriate lack of seriousness, overly casual

The joke added needed *levity* to the otherwise serious meeting.

Synonyms: amusement; humor

sin, evil act

"I promise to close every den of *iniquity* in this town!" thundered the conservative new mayor.

Synonyms: enormity; immorality; injustice; vice; wickedness

**LEVITY**

noun (leh vih tee)

## INNOCUOUS

adj (ih nahk yoo uhs)

acting in an indifferent or slow, sluggish manner

The clerk was so *lethargic* that, even when business was slow, he always had a long line in front of him.

Synonyms: apathetic; lackadaisical; languid; listless; torpid

harmless

Some snakes are poisonous, but most species are *innocuous* and pose no danger to humans.

Synonyms: benign; harmless; inoffensive; insipid

**LETHARGIC**

adj (luh thar jik)

**INQUEST**

noun (ihn kwehst)

trickery

The little boy thought his *legerdemain* was working on his mother, but she in fact knew about every hidden toy and stolen cookie.

Synonyms: chicanery; conjuring

an investigation, an inquiry

The police chief ordered an *inquest* to determine what went wrong.

Synonyms: probe; quest; research

**LEGERDEMAIN**

noun (lehj uhr duh mayn)

## INSIPID

adj (in sih pid)

suspicious

After being swindled once, Ruth became *leery* of strangers trying to sell things to her.

Synonyms: distrustful; guarded; wary

lacking interest or flavor

The critic claimed that the painting was *insipid*, containing no interesting qualities at all.

Synonyms: banal; bland; dull; stale; vapid

**LEERY**

adj (lihr ree)

# INSURRECTION

noun (ihn suh rehk shuhn)

extremely generous or extravagant

Olga gave her puppy so many *lavish* treats that it soon became overweight and spoiled.

Synonyms: extravagant; exuberant; luxuriant; opulent; prodigal; profuse; superabundant

rebellion

After the Emperor's troops crushed the *insurrection*, its leaders fled the country.

Synonyms: mutiny; revolt; revolution; uprising

**LAVISH**

adj (laa vish)

## INTER

verb (ihn <u>tuhr</u>)

to give praise, to glorify

Parades and fireworks were staged to *laud* the success of the rebels.

Synonyms: acclaim; applaud; commend; compliment; exalt; extol; hail; praise

to bury

After giving the masses one last chance to pay their respects, the leader's body was *interred*.

Synonyms: entomb; inhume; sepulchre; tomb

**LAUD**

verb (lawd)

## INTERREGNUM

noun (in tuh reg nuhm)

potential that is not readily apparent

*Latent* trait testing seeks to identify skills that the test taker may have that they are not aware of.

Synonyms: concealed; dormant; inert; potential; quiescent

interval between reigns

When John F. Kennedy was shot, there was a brief *interregnum* before Lyndon B. Johnson became president.

**LATENT**

adj (lāy tnt)

## INTRACTABLE

adj (ihn <u>traak</u> tuh buhl)

a state of diminished energy

The lack of energy that characterizes patients with anemia makes *lassitude* one of the primary symptoms of the disease.

Synonyms: debilitation; enervation; fatigue; languor; listlessness; tiredness; weariness

not easily managed or manipulated

*Intractable* for hours, the wild horse eventually allowed the rider to mount.

Synonyms: stubborn; unruly

**LASSITUDE**

noun (laas ih tood)

generous giving (as of money) to others who may seem inferior

She'd always relied on her parent's *largess*, but after graduation she had to get a job.

Synonyms: benevolence; boon; compliment; favor; present

## INTRANSIGENT

adj (ihn traan suh juhnt) (ihn traan zuh juhnt)

uncompromising, refusing to be reconciled

The professor was *intransigent* on the deadline, insisting that everyone turn in the assignment at the same time.

Synonyms: implacable; inexorable; irreconcilable; obdurate; obstinate; remorseless; rigid; unbending; unrelenting; unyielding

**LARGESS**

noun (laar jehs)

## INTREPID

adj (ihn treh pihd)

theft of property

The crime of stealing a wallet can be categorized as petty *larceny.*

Synonyms: burglary; robbery; stealing

fearless, resolutely courageous

Despite freezing winds, the *intrepid* hiker completed his ascent.

Synonym: brave

**LARCENY**

noun (laar suh nee)

**INUNDATE**

verb (<u>ih</u> nuhn dayt)

relating to precious stones or the art of cutting them

Most *lapidary* work today is done with the use of motorized equipment.

to overwhelm; to cover with water

The tidal wave *inundated* Atlantis, which was lost beneath the water.

Synonyms: deluge; drown; engulf; flood; submerge

**LAPIDARY**

adj (laa puh der ee)

## INURE

verb (ih <u>nyoor</u>)

lacking energy, slow; indifferent

The *languid* cat cleaned its fur, ignoring the vicious, snarling dog chained a few feet away from it.

Synonyms: fainéant; lackadaisical; listless; sluggish; weak

to harden; accustom, become used to

Eventually, Hassad became *inured* to the sirens that went off every night and could sleep through them.

Synonyms: condition; familiarize; habituate

**LANGUID**

adj (laang gwihd)

**INVECTIVE**

noun (ihn vek tihv)

to ridicule with satire

The mayor hated being *lampooned* by the press for his efforts to improve people's politeness.

Synonym: tease

abusive language

> A stream of *invectives* poured from Mrs. Pratt's mouth as she watched the vandals smash her ceramic frog.

Synonyms: denunciation; revilement; vituperation

**LAMPOON**

verb (laam poon)

## INVESTITURE

noun (in <u>ves</u> tuh chur)

to express sorrow, to grieve

The children continued to *lament* the death of the goldfish weeks after its demise.

Synonyms: bewail; deplore; grieve; mourn

ceremony conferring authority

At Napoleon's *investiture*, he grabbed the crown from the Pope's hands and placed it on his head himself.

Synonyms: inaugural; inauguration; induction; initiation; installation

**LAMENT**

verb (luh mehnt)

## INVIDIOUS

adj (ihn <u>vihd</u> ee uhs)

using few words

He was the classic *laconic* native of Maine; he talked as if he were being charged for each word.

Synonyms: concise; curt; pithy; taciturn; terse

envious, obnoxious, offensive; likely to promote ill-will

It is cruel and *invidious* for parents to play favorites with their children.

Synonyms: discriminatory; insulting; jaundiced; resentful

**LACONIC**

adj (luh kah nihk)

## IRASCIBLE

adj (ih rah suh buhl)

tearful

Marcella always became *lachrymose* when it was time to bid her daughter good-bye.

Synonyms: teary; weepy

easily made angry

> Attilla the Hun's *irascible* and violent nature made all who dealt with him fear for their lives.

Synonyms: cantankerous; irritable; ornery; testy

**LACHRYMOSE**

adj (laak ruh mohs)

## ITINERANT

adj (ie <u>tihn</u> uhr uhnt)

fame, glory, honor

The actress happily accepted *kudos* from the press for her stunning performance in the film.

Synonyms: acclaim; accolade; encomium; homage; praise

wandering from place to place; unsettled

The *itinerant* tomcat came back to the Johansson homestead every two months.

Synonyms: nomadic; vagrant

**KUDOS**

noun (koo dohz)

**JARGON**

noun (<u>jahr</u> guhn)

sound of a funeral bell; omen of death or failure

When the townspeople heard the *knell* from the church belfry, they knew that their mayor had died.

Synonyms: chime; peal; toll

nonsensical talk; specialized language

> You need to master technical *jargon* in order to communicate successfully with engineers.

Synonyms: argot; cant; dialect; idiom; slang

**KNELL**

noun (nehl)

## JETTISON

verb (jeht ih zuhn) (jeht ih suhn)

relating to motion; characterized by movement

The *kinetic* sculpture moved back and forth, startling the museum visitors.

Synonyms: active; dynamic; mobile

to discard, to get rid of as unnecessary or encumbering

The sinking ship *jettisoned* its cargo in a desperate attempt to reduce its weight.

Synonyms: dump; eject

**KINETIC**

adj (kih neh tihk)

# JINGOISM

noun (<u>jing</u> goh ihz uhm)

to set fire to or ignite; excite or inspire

With only damp wood to work with, Tilda had great difficulty trying to *kindle* the camp fire.

Synonyms: arouse; awaken; light; spark

belligerent support of one's country

The professor's *jingoism* made it difficult for the students to participate in an open political discussion.

Synonyms: chauvinism; nationalism

**KINDLE**

verb (kihn duhl)

## JOCULAR

adj (<u>jahk</u> yuh luhr)

having a sharp edge; intellectually sharp, perceptive

With her *keen* intelligence, she figured out the puzzle in seconds flat.

Synonyms: acute; canny; quick

playful, humorous

The *jocular* old man entertained his grandchildren for hours.

Synonyms: amusing; comical

**KEEN**

adj (keen)

## JUDICIOUS

adj (joo dih shuhs)

point of time, especially where two things are joined

At this *juncture*, I think it would be a good idea for us to take a coffee break.

Synonyms: confluence; convergence; crisis; crossroads; moment

sensible, showing good judgment

> The wise and distinguished judge was well known for having a *judicious* temperament.

Synonyms: circumspect; prudent; sagacious; sapient

**JUNCTURE**

noun (juhnk chuhr)

# NOTES

# NOTES

# NOTES

# NOTES

# NOTES